THE HEART
OF THE LAKES

The Heart of the Lakes

Freshwater in the Past, Present, and Future of Southeast Michigan

Dave Dempsey

Greenstone Books | *East Lansing*

♾ The paper used in this publication meets the minimum requirements
of ANSI/NISO Z39.48-1992 (R 1997) (Permanence of Paper).

Made possible by grants from the Community Foundation
of Southeast Michigan and Heritage Michigan

The Michigan Department of Natural Resources is committed to the
conservation, protection, management, use and enjoyment of the state's
natural and cultural resources for current and future generations.
Visit the DNR at *http://www.michigan.gov/dnr.*

Greenstone Books is an imprint of Michigan State University Press.
The mission of Greenstone Books—a name chosen to evoke
the state gem of Michigan—is to publish works in history and
environmental studies accessible to a general readership.

Michigan State University Press
East Lansing, Michigan 48823-5245

Printed and bound in the United States of America.

28 27 26 25 24 23 22 21 20 19   1 2 3 4 5 6 7 8 9 10

Library of Congress Control Number: 2018952426
Paper ISBN: 978-1-948314-04-6
PDF ISBN: 978-1-948314-05-3
ePub ISBN: 978-1-948314-06-0
Mobi/prc ISBN: 978-1-948314-07-7

Book design by Charlie Sharp, Sharp Des!gns, East Lansing, Michigan
Cover design by Erin Kirk New
Cover image is of the Gateway to Freedom International Memorial to the
Underground Railroad located in the Hart Plaza on the shore of the Detroit River,
sculpted by Ed Dwight and dedicated 20 October 2001.

Michigan State University Press is a member of the Green Press Initiative and is
committed to developing and encouraging ecologically responsible publishing
practices. For more information about the Green Press Initiative and the use of
recycled paper in book publishing, please visit *www.greenpressinitiative.org.*

Visit Michigan State University Press at *www.msupress.org*

To my brothers Jack and Tom
Gifted, ever loyal idealists and friends

For Native people, caring for the water is not merely a matter of practicality. We lived as human beings on this earth for thousands of years without relying on oil. We can live without gold. But *we cannot live without water.*

FRANK ETTAWAGESHIK, *Little Traverse Bay Bands of Odawa Indians*

Have you also learned that secret from the river; that there is no such thing as time? That the river is everywhere at the same time, at the source and at the mouth, at the waterfall, at the ferry, at the current, in the ocean and in the mountains, everywhere and that the present only exists for it, not the shadow of the past nor the shadow of the future.

HERMAN HESSE

CONTENTS

FOREWORD

Congressman John Dingell

A long letter is not needed here.

Let us first thank our author, the Community Foundation for Southeast Michigan who supported his effort, the others who have helped tell us so wise and valuable a tale, and the many others who have worked so long and so hard to preserve and protect our ecology, whose root word literally translates from the Greek word for "home." These people at no small cost to themselves have helped us preserve what we have of a beautiful world, in thousands of fights.

This book is about the heart of the Great Lakes, southeast Michigan: its settlement, development, abuse, recovery, and, now, its preservation. Similar histories could be written of all the continents and islands of our world. Perhaps this story will tell us how to do better in passing our trust to coming generations—as my dear dad taught me, we borrow this beautiful world from generations yet to come.

One of my dad's favorite stories kept running through my mind as I considered how to introduce this valuable, important work. Two men, one a city fellow and the other his friend and contemporary from the wilderness, visited each other's residences.

The city fellow, seeing the woods, open spaces, wildlife, and pure water gushed, "O Heaven!"

The woodsman, seeing all the filth, poverty, suffering, disease, and crowding in the city, exclaimed, "O Hell!"

That is what we have for too long done to God's great gifts of nature. Our care and custody of the treasures he has given to mankind are not what they could—or should—be.

These treasures are threatened by our use and misuse. Let us not deceive ourselves: shortsighted misuse and squandering of our resources threaten comfort and safety and the very world for future generations.

In front of the National Archives Building in Washington, DC, are the words "What is past is prologue." Let us take our warning while there is still time for us to change. We must get busy. All of us.

PREFACE

One of the first Europeans to reach the Great Lakes and write about it, in 1615, had profoundly failed: he had not found the Pacific Ocean, or an immediate and ready path to it, or access to its coveted wealth. What Samuel Champlain had found, though, was one of a series of conjoined "freshwater seas" that were evergreen sources of life and "springwells of imagination."[1] Champlain's "discovery" would prove to be more advantageous than his original objective. Today, the fresh water he found is a bigger treasure than the riches he pursued.

The natural resources inherent to the Great Lakes basin have always provided multiple benefits. A burgeoning fur trade drew explorers and settlers to this part of New France. Plentiful fish stocks offered sustenance to human life as they had for the indigenous people.

The water itself fueled the rapid industrial growth of southeast Michigan in the late 1800s and the first half of the twentieth century, and played an indispensable role in the region's cultural history. A boundary as well as a meeting point, the Detroit River helped usher former slaves to freedom from antebellum America and ferried bootlegged liquor to America during Prohibition. It served as a shipping superhighway, transporting both raw and refined materials to the Detroit area for use in manufacturing. It also served as a convenient sewer.

By the early 1900s, the waters of the St. Clair and Detroit Rivers were lethal. Thousands of Michiganders and Ontarians died because the municipal water they drank was drawn from rivers choked with raw sewage. Typhoid and cholera bred in those sewage-laden waters.

In the same age, communities up and down the two rivers and on the shores of Lake St. Clair forgot that these aquatic resources had values other than strictly utilitarian. Their beauty, which had a natural charm, was often blemished by industrial blight. In other cases, communities simply turned their backs to the water, failing to realize that they were sacrificing an environmental *and* economic asset.

This could not last. In the 1960s, the turnaround began. Water's use as a receptacle for foul and sometimes untreated municipal and industrial waste helped generate a public clamor for pollution control. The sorry spectacle of the Rouge and Detroit Rivers catching fire was merely the most dramatic expression of the collective insult to the region's water. Anticipating, not simply responding to federal mandates, Michigan enacted tougher water pollution control laws, and voters approved substantial funding for sewage cleanup. Within a handful of years—by 1980—the difference was palpable.

Although some problems (and some toxic pollutants) persist, the water is noticeably cleaner, and fish—including the magnificent Jurassic species the lake sturgeon—are reproducing at healthy rates.

Now, as communities up and down the Detroit River and its tributaries seek to renew their stewardship of water as a seminal attribute of heritage, character, and sustainable development, fresh water could resume its place as the key to the future in the heart of the Great Lakes region.

The challenge remains monumental—not solely physical, but also managerial. Late in 2015, a Michigan city became the focus of national attention when its freshwater supply failed. Residents of Flint had been exposed to above-normal levels of lead in their drinking water. It was not the fault of the source water, the Flint River, but of a failure to apply standard corrosion control protocols to this new supply.

Science and human judgment failed. As one newspaper put it, "A bureaucratic mess turned public-health disaster" created an "epic blunder" that may forever be known as the "Flint Water Crisis."[2]

Southeast Michigan can afford no such catastrophes. Its chance to chart a sustainable future with water at the center depends on planning that anticipates all contingencies, administration free of hubris, and perpetual vigilance.

This book travels down the water trail that defines southeast Michigan, occasionally paddling upriver in place and time, tracing history's ebb and flow, leading to the confluence of past and future. This virtual water journey also seeks to stimulate a conversation about the critical importance of action by the leaders and communities of southeast Michigan, and a glimpse at what those actions might be.

The region's future will require capital for fresh water and fresh ideas, innovation and talent, and pulling people together from all over the region and state. It will require widespread recognition that Michigan is poised, both in resources and in time, to become a hub for dealing with humanity's water challenges—if it acts now.

A prosperous future will require a passage from complacency to commitment to a conviction that southeast Michigan can show the world the way to nurturing the water that all of life requires.

We are all made of water; we all have a common interest in water. For a region that has often splintered along demographic lines, water has the potential to foster unity. But only if there is a common plan—and actions that flow from it.

This is a story of development, exploitation, decline, and rebuilding—and a fateful choice in the immediate future. That choice: allow events to control southeast Michigan's water destiny, or harness a community vision and energies to catapult the region to international water resource leadership.

ACKNOWLEDGMENTS

A To Paul Dimond, Mariam Noland, and the Community Foundation for Southeast Michigan for the vision and funding to make the manuscript possible.

To Sandra Sageser Clark, Michigan Historical Center, for overseeing its undertaking.

To the Michigan Historical Commission for its sponsorship and its devout leadership and participation in preservation and promotion of our state's heritage.

To the Michigan Legislature of 1955 and Governor G. Mennen Williams for their foresight in enacting the law that created the Michigan Historical Marker Program, without which this work would have been virtually impossible.

To the Michigan Environmental Council, Michigan Department of Natural Resources, and Michigan Historical Commission for their decadelong work to create for Michigan's citizens and visitors the Conservation Heritage Marker Trail.

To repositories of books and periodicals throughout Michigan, including the Bentley Historical Library, Clarke Historical Library at Central Michigan University, Library of Michigan, and Michigan eLibrary.

To the many women and men who have contributed knowledge and passion to the restoration of the waters of southeast Michigan.

To Jack Dempsey, president of the Michigan Historical Commission and brother of the author, for his encouragement and support in the preparation of this manuscript.

THE HEART
OF THE LAKES

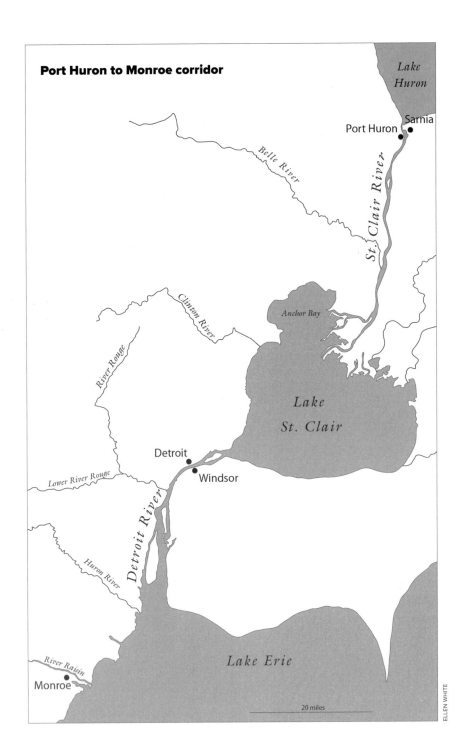

Port Huron to Monroe corridor

Lake Huron

Sarnia
Port Huron

Belle River

St. Clair River

Clinton River

Anchor Bay

River Rouge

Lake St. Clair

Detroit

Lower River Rouge

Windsor

Detroit River

Huron River

Lake Erie

River Raisin

Monroe

20 miles

ELLEN WHITE

CHAPTER 1

Where the Water Came From

The Laurentian Great Lakes were formed nearly 20,000 years ago when the earth's climate warmed and the last glacial continental ice sheet retreated. The glacier, up to 2 miles thick, was so heavy and powerful it gouged out the earth's surface to create the lake basins. Meltwater from the retreating glacier filled the newly created basins. Approximately 3,500–4,000 years ago, the Great Lakes attained their modern levels and area.

—National Oceanic and Atmospheric Administration,
Great Lakes Environmental Research Laboratory

Measured by the span of a human lifetime, the heart of the lakes is ancient. In geological terms, it is an infant. Perhaps five hundred generations have passed since people resettled the Great Lakes watershed following the end of the last glaciations. That translates to approximately 10,000 years, about 0.000002222 percent of the earth's age of approximately 4.5 billion years. Geologically, the glaciers didn't leave yesterday, they left this morning.

The Great Lakes visible from space and maps looked much different when a smothering blanket of ice finally withdrew ten millennia ago. First exposed were Lake Chicago (now southern Lake Michigan) and Lake Erie. Both drained southwest to the Mississippi River. A thousand years after, the young Lake Superior, termed Lake Duluth by scientists, also drained into the Mississippi watershed.

Another two thousand years passed. The land southwest of Lake Erie rebounded from the weight of the departed glacier, blocking the lake's outflow, directing it over what became Niagara Falls, and creating Lake Ontario. The glacier withdrew into Canada, pooling Lakes Michigan, Huron, and Superior into giant Lake Nippissing. Water levels then fell, creating the three water bodies whose borders closely resemble those we know. Lake Huron continued to drain out via the Ottawa River to the St. Lawrence River until between five and six thousand years ago. Then the fateful happened. As the land to the north and northeast rose, the old outlet of Lake Huron through North Bay was closed off, and the pressure of Lake Huron forced its drainage through what is now the St. Clair River.

Today the St. Clair spills a peak flow of around 230,000 cubic feet per second from a drainage area of 224,000 square miles. At the river's origin its peak velocity can approach four miles per hour, eight times faster than the Ohio River at Pittsburgh. The St. Clair also links with its namesake lake and the Detroit River, placing southeast Michigan at the center of the world's largest freshwater system.

Who were the first Great Lakes explorers and settlers? The first peoples are thought to have arrived from the west a little more than ten thousand years ago. Archaeological evidence demonstrates that a group of aboriginals established a seasonal camp near what is now Traverse City around 8300 BCE. Six thousand years ago they had settled throughout the Great Lakes region. They hunted, fished, grew staples such as corn and squash, and harvested wild rice. Tobacco assumed prominence in tribal cultures, leading by 1000 BCE to tubular smoking pipes.

Water was the neighborhood in which many indigenous villages located.

Rivers provided transportation and an abundant food supply. These first peoples mined copper from the Keweenaw Peninsula and Isle Royale. They established sophisticated trading networks reaching hundreds or thousands of miles in all directions.

When Europeans arrived, the heart of the lakes included visible traces of human heritage in mounds built by the indigenous peoples. These mounds were often found along watercourses. Mounds flanked the St. Clair River at what is now Port Huron, and a cluster of four mounds stood along the Detroit River at present-day Fort Wayne. But the largest was the Great Mound of the River Rouge, not far from the Rouge's mouth at the Detroit River. Estimated at two hundred feet long, three hundred feet wide, and twenty feet tall, it was a landmark for the early Europeans. Like almost all of the mounds in the region, it was pillaged and flattened by the new arrivals. Although this mound contained human bones as well as artifacts like arrowheads, not all of the mounds were burial sites. Some contained only pottery, utensils, and weapons.

At the time of European contact in 1620, the population of what is now Michigan totaled about fifteen thousand. The southern half of the Lower Peninsula accounted for about twelve thousand. Both cultures venerated the vast freshwater seas. Containing six quadrillion gallons of water, 18 percent of the available surface fresh water on earth, the Great Lakes are indeed a gift of the glaciers. Annual rainfall and snowmelt supply only 1 percent of the volume of the Great Lakes. The remaining 99 percent of the volume is the legacy of the Ice Age. The small fraction associated with current-day events means the Great Lakes are vulnerable to changes in climate as well as the vagaries of human uses of their water.

Fed by the waters of three of the largest lakes in the world, southeast Michigan's most dramatic natural feature is the water passage constituted by the Detroit and St. Clair Rivers and the lake between them, a natural highway connecting the upper and lower Great Lakes. The hundred-mile adjacent stretch of lake plain from Port Huron to Monroe is intersected by six tributary rivers that all flow eastward into this passage. The sources of these six great inland-originating rivers—the Black, the Belle, the Clinton, the Rouge, the Huron, and the Raisin—shape an "emerald arc" at the fringe of southeast Michigan, with the Detroit River forming the diagonal of the mighty bow.

For southeast Michiganders, water is an integral part of the character of home. Often forgotten because they are embedded in the everyday, water's geography, hydrology, scenery, and history are central to the heart of the lakes and a key to community life. The feel of southeast Michigan is inextricably linked with these waterways. The region's inhabitants would not know where they are without the familiar freshwater landmarks all around them.

CHAPTER 2

The Headwaters

She stood on the piazza in the almost paralyzing bitterness, looking down at Blue River. Under that ice it flowed—endomed yet living, breathing; a core of beauty, an indispensable link in these great waterways. Blue River, the one changeless thing in her life . . . It was not just a stream marking a boundary line and connecting the Great Lakes waterways. It was a friend who shared the happenings of her days. In the light of the rising sun its awesome wonder could almost still the beat of her heart, and with evening its proud gray face withdrew into a friendly eternity and made of darkness a promise rather than a mystery.

—Mary Frances Doner, *Blue River*, 1946[1]

The waterways were for the aboriginal peoples a common property—or, perhaps more accurately, the subject of no one's ownership. Instead, the beneficence of creation made it possible for Native Americans to survive, to thrive, and to pass their wisdom on.

When the United States was still newly independent, before millions

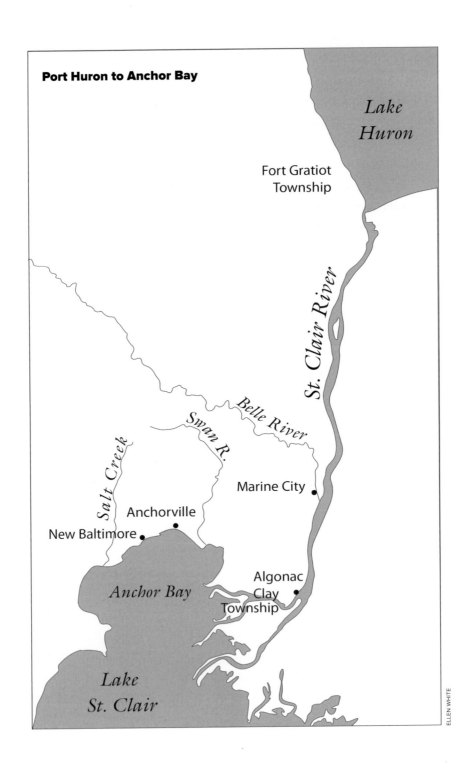

Port Huron to Anchor Bay

Lake
Huron

Fort Gratiot
Township

St. Clair River

Belle River

Swan R.

Salt Creek

Marine City

Anchorville

New Baltimore

Anchor Bay

Algonac
Clay
Township

Lake
St. Clair

ELLEN WHITE

of people descended on the region in search of a bountiful life, lawmakers made an important policy statement in some ways comparable in values to those of the aboriginal inhabitants. Recognizing the preciousness of the watercourses in the Great Lakes, Congress declared:

> The navigable waters leading into the . . . St. Lawrence, and the carrying places between the same, shall be common highways and forever free, as well to the inhabitants of the said territory as to the citizens of the United States, and those of any other States that may be admitted into the confederacy, without any tax, impost, or duty therefor.[2]

The waters of southeast Michigan, as of the Great Lakes system, have lived up to the pronouncement of "forever free." As a commons, these waters are for all to use—and for all to guard. Few kayakers, canoeists, or passengers or pilots of motorized pleasure craft are likely aware of the Northwest Ordinance or the public trust doctrine—an element of common law that obligates government to protect the public value of resources such as water that are shared by all—but these legal protections support their freedom to use the St. Clair River. And that is where this narrative begins its journey.

Traveling downstream from the mouth of Lake Huron makes sense not only because this is the direction of the swift current, but also because the early European explorers typically arrived in what is now southeast Michigan not from the south but from the north. The earliest, the French, canoed from Montreal up the Ottawa River, into the Mattawa River, across Lake Nipissing, and into the French River, which empties into Georgian Bay.

Once the voyageurs made their reports, it became obvious to the French government that there was great strategic advantage in controlling the water route from Lake Huron to Lake Erie. In summer 1701, a one-hundred-man party under Sieur Antoine de la Mothe Cadillac found passage through the St. Clair River. Departing the French River and moving along the shore of Georgian Bay, they made their way steadily southward, "over to Lake Huron, down through the St. Clair River and lake, and on to the lower river, where

[Cadillac] built Fort Pontchartrain and founded the city of Detroit," more properly "La Ville d'Etroit"—city of the strait.[3] Cadillac came for advantage and wealth. He became enraptured with the locale and its "sweet water." He appreciated not just the site of the new city, but the entire Huron-to-Erie corridor:

> Detroit is a river lying north-north-east towards Lake Huron and south-south-west to the entrance of Lake Erie. According to my reckoning it will be about 25 or 26 leagues in length and it is navigable throughout so that a vessel of 100 guns could pass through it safely.
>
> Towards the middle there is a lake which has been called St. Claire, which is about 30 leagues in circumference and 10 leagues in length. This lake is scarcely noticed, on account of several large and fine islands which form various passages or channels which are no wider than the river. It is only for about four leagues that the channel is wider . . .
>
> At the entrance to Lake Huron the lands are brown and well wooded; a vast and grand prairie is seen there which extends to the interior of the lands on both sides of the river up to Lake St. Claire, there are fewer prairies than elsewhere.
>
> All the surroundings of this lake are extensive pasture lands, and the grass on them is so high that a man can scarcely be seen in it.
>
> This river or strait of the seas is scattered over, from one lake to the other, both on the mainland and on the islands there, in its plains and on its banks, with large clusters of trees surrounded by charming meadows; but these same trees are marvelously lofty, without nodes and almost without branches until near the top, except the great oak.
>
> On the banks and round about the clusters of timber there is an infinite number of fruit trees, chiefly plums and apples. They are so well laid out that they might be taken for orchards planted by the hand of a gardener.[4]

The bounty and the beauty and the waters would distinguish what is now southeast Michigan from all other places on Earth.

⌐⌐

A potential northern put-in point for a kayaker or canoeist seeking to travel the St. Clair River corridor is a small, lakeshore park about five miles north of Port Huron. Coincidentally, offshore from this public space, a disaster associated with the fresh water of southeast Michigan took place. On the afternoon of Saturday, December 11, 1971, a powerful explosion reverberated through a tunnel excavated six miles out beneath Lake Huron. The blast scattered a crew of forty-three men working one mile from the head of the tunnel, 250 feet below the surface.[5]

A volunteer firefighter from a nearby department who arrived early on the scene said, "It looked like an H-Bomb hit that tunnel."[6] One of the workers, twenty-four-year-old Larry Verner, told a reporter that the explosion's shock wave "picked me up and threw me about 10 feet through the air." He was one of the fortunate. Verner's father and brother were not. Working farther down the tunnel and closer to the source of the blast, both were killed. The explosion hurled a fifteen-ton piece of equipment one-third of a mile. In all, twenty-two men, ranging in age from twenty to sixty-three, perished. It was one of the worst workplace disasters in Michigan's history.

What killed these men, and what had they been doing?

They were constructing an intake tunnel to serve metropolitan Detroit and northern suburbs with a new source of clean, fresh drinking water. In the 1950s, envisioning expansion of the population into the foreseeable future, planners concluded that an intake supplementing the existing one in the Detroit River could support the northern zone of the Detroit Water and Sewerage District service area, including Flint. The waters of Huron were tantamount to gold, said the head of the district, because they were so clean.

Detailed planning began in 1962 for a sixteen-foot-diameter intake tunnel, more than two hundred feet below the lakebed, and drawing up to 1.2 billion gallons of raw water per day from the lake. Construction began in 1968. It proceeded smoothly, for the most part, until the day of the accident in December 1971. A communication error left workers inside the shore end of the tunnel while a crew drilled through sediment at the other end. When a drill bit was dropped into methane gas released by the operation, it touched off a monstrous explosion, killing men more than four miles away.

Investigations and lawsuits followed. Laws strengthening workplace safety monitoring and enforcement took effect. Construction temporarily halted, then resumed, and the treatment plant receiving the intake water opened in 1974. In 2011, the plant pumped an average of 270 million gallons of water per day.

A visitor to Fort Gratiot County Park will find the two faces of the project on the two sides of a state historical marker. One side stresses the tragic human losses and the terrible power of the explosion: "[A] shotgun-like blast claimed the lives of twenty-two men working on a water intake tunnel beneath the bed of Lake Huron. A pocket of methane trapped within a layer of ancient Antrim shale fueled the explosion. An exhaustive inquiry determined that drilling for a vertical ventilation shaft from the lake's surface had released the trapped gas. . . . The blast created a shock wave with a speed of 4,000 miles an hour and a force of 15,000 pounds per square inch. Witnesses reported seeing debris fly 200 feet in the air from the tunnel's entrance."

The other side emphasizes the project itself: "In 1968, to serve the water needs of a growing population, the Detroit Metro Water Department began work on the Lake Huron Water Supply Project. This massive feat involved erecting a submerged intake crib connected to a six-mile intake tunnel beneath Lake Huron. The mechanical mole that dug the 16-foot wide tunnel bored through the bedrock beneath the lake at a rate of 150 feet a day. The project excavated more than one billion pounds of rock. The water treatment plant pumped clean water into an 82-mile system of water mains supplying Detroit and Flint. When finished in 1973, the $123 million system boasted a capacity of 400 million gallons a day."

Nearby, the nearly life-size bronze statue of a tunnel worker, and the names of the victims engraved in stone, inspire somber contemplation. On summer days, the happy cries of children playing in the park's Lake Huron surf are easily audible from beside the statue.

As the 1971 tunnel disaster proves, sometimes the cost of clean water is priced in human lives. Especially in light of the sacrifice made by twenty-two men, the value of southeast Michigan's public water supply should never be taken for granted.

⌐

Beginning just south of Fort Gratiot County Park, paddlers are making use of a system of water trails that ultimately lace the corridor from St. Clair River to the Detroit River corridor together. The Blueways of St. Clair, one of eight clusters of water trails in southeast Michigan, offers sixteen routes, supported by the St. Clair County Metropolitan Planning Commission and the St. Clair County Parks and Recreation Commission.[7] Paddlers choosing the Blue Water Bridges Excursion are encouraged to put in upstream of the Blue Water Bridges, where lake ends and river begins.[8] "The shoreline is developed, but the water is clean and blue," the Blueways website advises. But it also has a warning: "Use extreme caution when paddling under the Blue Water Bridges! The current is very strong and there can be substantial wave action." It also advises against paddling near the bridges on a weekend after noon, thanks to the mass of powerboat traffic.

Soon lake meets river. Huron water crowds inside the St. Clair, a thirty-nine-mile waterway that replenishes Lake St. Clair. A swift current moves at an average of 3.3 miles per hour at medium water flow, ushering 188,000 cubic feet per second of water downstream near the head of the river.

The strategic value of the freshwater throttle at the narrow end of Lake Huron drew the French to build a settlement here in the late 1600s.[9] In 1686 the French explorer Daniel Greysolon, Sieur du Lhut (anglicized to Duluth) constructed Fort St. Joseph to guard the upper end of the waterway joining Lakes Erie and Huron. In 1687, the fort was the mobilization center for a war party of French and Indians, but the threat of immediate conflict faded and a change in command led to the fort's abandonment in 1688.

The US government recognized the strategic importance of the site after the War of 1812 as the nation was securing its borders. A federal stockade was built in 1814 and later named Fort Gratiot after Charles Gratiot, the US Army Corps engineer supervising its construction. Gratiot had journeyed up the river to the old site of Fort St. Joseph, and here he decided to erect the stockade. It was "on the west shore of the St. Clair River about 1,000 feet below the narrow entrance from the lake to the river and on the high bank separated from the water's edge by a few yards of low sandy ground."[10] The site was garrisoned intermittently for much of the nineteenth century.

One colorful account from the early 1830s describes a rather rustic and rudimentary military settlement. An officer of the First Royal Regiment out of London, Ontario, paid a visit to Fort Gratiot in 1842. He "put up at 'The Hotel,' a dirty pot-house full of wild-looking roughs." After retiring, the soldier was accosted by an American dissatisfied with the state of US-Canadian relations and was told to clear out. He did so with alacrity.[11]

In 1820, American explorer and ethnologist Henry Rowe Schoolcraft rode the St. Clair River north by canoe. The scene evoked his admiration. "It is difficult to imagine," he observed, "a more delightful prospect, than is presented by this strait." His account helped dispel notions that southern Michigan was an inhospitable frontier. Those who made this journey, he wrote,

> in an earlier day found their chief interest in the primeval setting—the broad stream shimmering in the sunlight, the marshy areas where green rushes waved in the breeze, the deep dark forests bordering the banks and extending far inland.[12]

In 1825 construction began on the Fort Gratiot Light nearby. After a violent storm damaged it, Congress appropriated funds to build a more solid structure. Completed in 1829, the tower stands just north of the Blue Water Bridges, a sentinel in storm and sun for nearly two centuries, still warning mariners of the end of the lake. The structure is composed of conical brick, and a seven-building complex on the site, constructed from 1829 to 1939, is listed on the National Register of Historic Places. It is the oldest surviving lighthouse in Michigan, standing on the foundation of the first lighthouse in the state.

The first visitors to this area from the American East sought opportunity. They "came to the river and saw possibilities of acquiring wealth in lumbering, shipbuilding and trade." Once roots were sunk, though, a more domestic scene characterized life on the St. Clair River, as in this account written shortly after the War of 1812: "It is delightful to gaze upon the succession of dwellings, low and roomy, which its western bank presents, embowered in orchards, the children playing under the far-spreading elms, and the cattle grazing in rich meadows."[13]

Early maps of the area show a small community known as "Gratiot" with few streets. The lighthouse marks the shoreline as the lake terminates at the river; the fort protects the narrows several hundred feet south of that point. The Sarnia side is virtually unpopulated. Despite its "port" location, there was no harbor per se that welcomed vessels seeking a safe dock. Still, the idea of a haven at the end of the descent on the second largest of the Great Lakes was pleasing. Ships nearing the "welcome beacon" were no longer at overwhelming risk of imminent death in a great storm.[14]

The easternmost point in Michigan—as far east as Greenville, South Carolina—Port Huron today is the location for fourteen sites on the National Register of Historic Places and seventeen Michigan historical markers. It is also the starting line for the one of two famed long-distance freshwater competitions on the Great Lakes. The first annual Port Huron–to–Mackinac Island race began on July 25, 1925. The competing vessels were towed from Lake St. Clair up the St. Clair River to the starting line at Port Huron. Twelve boats began the 261-mile race to Mackinac Island, but only six finished. Today, hundreds compete in several classes.

At the mouth of the Black River is the Great Lakes Maritime Center. The home of boatnerd.com, a source of information on Great Lakes shipping including a map of vessel locations, the center also harbors a live linkup to an underwater camera in the river revealing fish, including the recovering lake sturgeon population. It offers movies on maritime subjects, guest talks about maritime subjects, and an up-close view of the restless river.

Marysville

The journey downstream to Marysville is approximately five miles. Marysville is one of six Michigan communities that takes its drinking water from the St. Clair River. The city calls Great Lakes water "the most beautiful and cleanliest water in the Northern Hemisphere." Still, the river has not been immune to drinking water threats. At one time, chemical spills, especially from a complex of facilities along the river in Sarnia that constitutes approximately 40 percent of Canada's chemical industry, were common. With environmental agencies urging them on, the so-called Chemical Valley took precautions to reduce spills. But some continued to occur. In April 2016, the Sarnia Imperial Oil facility spilled hydrochloric acid in the river. Marysville officials said the acid did not show up in its test results.

Because of issues associated with drinking water, fish habitat, fish consumption, and other uses, a US-Canadian panel listed the St. Clair River as one of forty-three Great Lakes areas of concern in 1985. The listing brought with it concentrated effort and dedicated funding to restore all impaired uses of the river. As of 2016, the cleanup effort had restored five of ten impaired uses, with more expected to be restored in the near future.[15] In addition to the St. Clair River, the heart of the lakes includes four rivers that are designated as areas of concern: the Clinton, Rouge, River, and Raisin.

Marysville traces its history to 1786, when a pioneer built a sawmill. In 1817, Zephaniah W. Bunce sailed up the St. Clair River and settled at the place of the mill, immodestly naming it Bunce Creek. A later settler made his home at the present-day foot of Huron Boulevard and named his business Vickery's Landing; the settlement became known as Vicksburg. Since another town in Michigan by that name existed, in 1859 a change was made to Marysville after the spouse of one of the mill owners.

The Rise and Fall and Rise Again
of Drinking Water Monitoring

At one point, spills of hazardous substances into the St. Clair River regularly posed a threat to public health. The swift current of the river rapidly spread the toxins downstream, where several communities drew their drinking water. Municipalities sometimes shut their drinking water intakes until the threat passed. On other occasions, they never heard of the spill.

The 1980s were a particularly dangerous time. Spills "were almost a daily occurrence."[*] In 1985, Dow Chemical's Sarnia plant spilled nearly three thousand gallons of perchloroethylene, used as a solvent in dry cleaning and other applications, into the river. Because the chemical isn't soluble, the spill created what news media called a "toxic blob" on the bottom of the river.

Although spills were much reduced by the 2000s, they still occurred with enough frequency to warrant environmental monitoring. With federal and state dollars paying the bill, communities from Port Huron to Monroe were able in 2006 to install state-of-the-art water monitoring to spot spills in real time. Fourteen drinking water treatment facilities were able to detect and respond to leaks and spills. The water treatment plants supplied over 4 million residents and thousands of businesses, including many served by the Detroit Water and Sewerage District.

Computer driven, with mass spectrometers and gas chromatographs, the system analyzed water quality around the clock, sounding the alarm if it detected contamination. Detroit water officials selected more than one hundred contaminants they wanted quickly detected by the system's sensors and probes. The system provided data every fifteen to thirty minutes. The data were quickly posted on a public website.

Helping drive the startup of the system was a 2003 spill of vinyl chloride, a carcinogen, by Royal Polymers in Sarnia when a power outage hit the northeastern United States and parts of Canada. The spill went unreported for five days. Authorities were never able to pinpoint the size of the spill.

After the network commenced operation, the number of spills declined. US Representative Candice Miller, who obtained the federal money to support the network, said monitoring and public disclosure had a deterrent effect. In July 2011 changes detected by the monitors in the pH level on the upper St. Clair River forced the shutdown of the Port Huron water filtration plant. Discharges from a paper mill were blamed, and the monitoring system had proven its value.

Once federal and state money ran out, it was up to locals to supply funding for the system's $1.2 million annual budget. Supporters of the network called for a twenty-five-cent annual fee per household or business—rejected by several governments as a new tax. The City of St. Clair withdrew its support from the network in 2011, starting an exodus by multiple communities.

Representative Miller lamented the deterioration of the monitoring program. "Unfortunately, maintaining this system was not made a priority, and it eventually crumbled," she said. Referring to a 2016 spill, she observed, "We are reminded of the threat posed by such spills and of the need to revive a monitoring system that provides residents with the assurances they deserve."[+]

The vice president of the firm involved in overseeing the network, Jim Ridgway, said the collapse of the monitoring system showed that clean drinking water is too often taken for granted. "It was very short sighted," Ridgway said. "Communities are all under financial pressure and sometimes look at this type of monitoring as too costly to maintain. I would argue that the cost is small and the benefits are large."

Recognizing the benefits to public safety of the monitoring system, Governor Rick Snyder's administration revived it in 2018. A $375,000 grant from the state's infrastructure fund enabled fourteen communities in the Huron-to-Erie Drinking Water Protection Corridor to re-establish a network, linked by computer.[‡]

---

*David Gough, "Chemical Spills on St. Clair River Are Rare," *Wallaceburg Courier Press*, July 19, 2016, http://www.wallaceburgcourierpress.com/2016/07/19/chemical-spills-on-st-clair-river-are-rare.

†"Chemical Spill Revives Call for Real-Time Water Monitoring," *Macomb Daily*, April 23, 2016.

‡Jim Bloch, "Drinking water monitoring to relaunch along Huron-Erie corridor," *The Voice*, August 2, 2018, http://www.voicenews.com/life/drinking-water-monitoring-to-relaunch-along-huron-erie-corridor/article_c6cfe77a-bf69-5f5c-be41-4e99faf7c276.html.

The look of the area when Europeans arrived can only be imagined today. "The pine forest that stretched from Pine River to the Strait of Mackinac was barely touched by man. This was woodland. Eventually saw mills dotted the shorelines of streams in Marysville."[16]

St. Clair

Another six miles downstream is the city of St. Clair. One of its riverside landmarks is the St. Clair Inn, which opened in 1926 and was well known as a place of luxury and the perfect venue for freighter viewing. In 2016, it had been vacant two years and had fallen into disrepair. A developer acquired it early that year and vowed to restore its glory.

The inn's history traces to the pre-Depression era of great expectations. Pleasure craft were numerous on the St. Clair River early in the twentieth century. In 1925 community leaders agreed that a luxury establishment was needed to accommodate a growing number of tourists attracted by the water and its vessel traffic. At the same time, it would serve as a civic and social center. Opened in September 1926, the structure was listed on the National Register of Historic Places in 1995.

The city of St. Clair's history reaches back much farther than the inn's construction. In 1779, Jean Baptiste Point du Sable, a Haitian-born son of a French businessman and an African slave, was arrested and brought to British-governed Fort Michilimackinac on suspicion of being a French sympathizer. When the garrison commander discovered du Sable's skills as a trader and business person, he sent the captive to "The Pinery," on the south bank of the Pine River here, to manage it. Du Sable took care of the property until 1784, when he returned to his trading post in Chicago and helped found the city that is now the largest on the Great Lakes.[17]

St. Clair has ingeniously labeled itself the site of the world's longest freshwater boardwalk. Astride Palmer Park, the boardwalk offers intimate views of passing freighters.

Marine City

Seven more miles downstream is Marine City. Where Belle River meets the St. Clair, a town named Yankee Point was settled in 1820 when "lake captain Samuel Ward came here . . . and built his log house on what is now the main street."[18] He was not, by far, the first inhabitant. The Ojibwa had known this river junction for centuries before European contact.

The French were the first Europeans to claim it, their settlement marked, like Detroit to the south, by "ribbon farms" shaped like elongated rectangles moving away from the water with the narrow end along the riverfront. This land pattern enabled each farmer to have access to an endless supply of fresh water for agriculture and personal needs. After a succession of names, the village was incorporated as "Marine" in 1865. In 1867 it was renamed Marine City. The newly christened city was known as a shipbuilding center. Captains and sailors made their homes here. Indeed, the first chief executive of "Marine village" was a prominent shipbuilder. When wooden ships still reigned, Marine City was one of the largest shipbuilding centers in the Great Lakes area. Its output was nearly 250 vessels by 1900. With ready access to lumber and situated at a river junction, the community boomed as ship designers and fashioners combined to make it a freshwater boatbuilding Mecca.

Algonac

Eight miles farther south, Algonac is at the point where the St. Clair first splits into channels. Settled in 1805,[19] it endured a period of renaming until the community settled on Henry Schoolcraft's invention, intended to evoke the tradition and culture of the indigenous people: "Algon" from the Algonquin Indians, and "ac" as a helpful suffix.

Boatbuilding gave Algonac an identity; speed gave it fame, including the nickname "Water Speed Capital." The claim owes its origin to a Michigander who first brought home to Algonac the world title for motorboat racing. In 1903, Englishman Alfred Charles William Harmsworth, 1st Viscount Northcliffe, a tabloid publisher, thought to inspire international interest by founding the Harmsworth Cup, to be awarded to the vessel that motored over the water faster than any other. To his delight, England took home the first trophy with a head-spinning mark of nearly twenty miles per hour. An American boat won it in 1907, and the two nations alternated in taking it home until the end of World War I.

Garfield Arthur Wood (named for two US presidents) arrived on the scene. "Gar," as he was known, had been familiar with boats from childhood. In 1913 he founded the Wood Hydraulic Hoist & Body Company at 560 Franklin Street, one block south of East Jefferson Avenue and close by the Detroit River. His patented truck bodies and lifts were eagerly sought by the US Army during the preparations for and conduct of World War I. Now wealthy, he continued to expand the business and, most important, devote time and money to his powerboat hobby.

At a meeting of the Detroit Exchange Club in 1916, Wood had purchased the *Miss Detroit I* powerboat. He drove north to see the craft in the yards of the Chris Smith & Sons Boat Company in Algonac. Wood soon commissioned a new *Miss Detroit III* from the Smith boat works, purchased a controlling interest in the company, and made his summer residence at Algonac to oversee the design, construction, testing, and perfection of the vessel.

From 1917 to 1921, Smith and Wood together won five consecutive Gold Cups, the American powerboat speed trophy, and Wood took home first place in other competitions. In 1920 and 1921, Christopher Smith and Gar Wood won the Harmsworth trophy together. The second victory came early in a series of Miss America boats built in Algonac. The Miss Americas continued to bring home the Harmsworth trophy from 1922 to 1933. In 1932, the *Miss America X* established a world water speed record of 124.91 miles per hour. During the same years, Smith had founded the Chris-Craft Corporation to build pleasure craft and parted ways with Wood in 1923. The Algonac firm became one of the world's largest builders of power pleasure boats.

The origins of Chris-Craft go back to 1874, when Christopher Columbus Smith built his first boat at age thirteen at "Point du Chene," later Algonac. By 1927 the company was recognized as the world's largest builder of mahogany-constructed recreational powerboats. After helping win World War II by furnishing combat craft, Chris-Craft soon offered 139 different recreational models.

For years, Michigan held the distinction of selling the greatest number of boating licenses of any state, with the Algonac-based boatbuilding firm a major contributor. After various corporate changes, an investment group bought the company in 2001 and introduced a line of new Heritage models. In 2014 it launched a vertical bow series hearkening back 140 years to the predecessor company's beginnings along the St. Clair.

Gar Wood and Chris Smith are remembered fondly in Algonac. In 2010, a statue of the two was dedicated at Algonac City Park, the former site of the Chris-Craft factory.[20]

Harsen's Island

Approximately five miles farther along, the river becomes complicated nautically and ecologically. At the river's mouth is a delta emptying into Lake St. Clair, a natural feature classified as a "bird's foot" design, like the well-known Mississippi delta. It is the only major river delta in the Great Lakes. Seven active channels comprise the St. Clair delta; between the channels lie six major named islands.

North America's largest freshwater delta forms a hunting and fishing paradise and has been home to Native peoples for generations. Six islands in Canada—Bassett, Potawatomi, Seaway, Squirrel, St. Anne, and Walpole—are also known as the "St. Clair Flats," together with Dickinson Island, Harsens Island, and Russell Island on the Michigan side.[21] Cherished by the Walpole Island First Nations, comprised of Anishinaabe (the Ojibwa, Potawatomi, and Ottawa peoples), the area was dubbed Bkejwanong: "where the waters divide."

The Native river people have long appreciated their environment, and they have valuable traditional knowledge to share. The southeast Michigan watersheds remain "our home and our lifeblood." Where the waters divide is a "unique system of wetlands" defended and nurtured by "a strong cultural heritage that is celebrated by our people." They "bring to the table a willingness to share our knowledge which includes both our ways of knowing as well as the traditional values which are part and parcel of our understanding of how our watershed system works and how it can be enhanced as we move forward in the future together."[22]

This area also has a long history of European settlement. The first European to stay arrived during the American Revolution, built a log home, and set up his fur trade and gun business. After the cabin blew up from a powder mishap, Jacob Harsen built a better one. It was the family home from 1800 to the 1940s, situated at the north end of the island named after him.

Harsens Island sits at the end of the river, accessible only by ferry or private boat. About a thousand people live on the island full time. In recent years, the ferry operator has proposed terminating service. Residents have wondered aloud how they can remain on the island, and some of them hope for government intervention. The southern end of the island features the St. Clair Flats State Wildlife Area and both Little Muscamoot Bay and its Big companion. The latter is the site of the annual "raft off" on the first weekend of August, when thousands of recreational boaters tie off their craft in rows and indulge.

The relative isolation and strategic location of Harsens Island and the St. Clair Flats made the area a prime traffic corridor for alcohol transportation from Canada during Prohibition.[23] But the same isolation—and difficulty of developing marshy land—have long made the area a waterfowl hunting haven.

In May 1872, four Detroit sportsmen purchased a tract in the flats adjacent to Harsens Island and formed the St. Clair Fishing and Shooting Club of Detroit.[24] Plentiful fish and ducks distinguished the location. The founders built twenty-six boathouses and a clubhouse on stilts for $1,514.33. For the first sixty-eight years of its existence, access to the club was available only by water. Regular ferry service to the club was organized. By 1890 sportsmen could depart from the foot of Woodward Avenue in Detroit for a mere one-hour trip to the club. The Great Lakes steamer *Tashmoo* began service from Detroit to Port Huron, stopping at the club. In 1902, the club was reorganized as "The Old Club." The name seems more apt today as it nears its sesquicentennial. It is a place of long tradition. As the club puts it: "The lure of the open blue water is still one of the great assets of The Old Club, whether it is prowling the rivers and flats in search of the wily small mouth bass . . . or sitting on the boardwalk watching the spectacular boats pass."

A portion of St. Clair Flats is off-limits to hunting, but the remainder is a "premier public hunting area," according to Ducks Unlimited. Duck hunters will find mallards, black ducks, pintail, wood ducks, Canada geese, and several other species that are taken each year.

The flats occupy an important place in the state's aquatic legal history. Court battles over private ownership of submerged land in the delta led the

Michigan Supreme Court to declare in 1910 that the flats' bottomlands were public lands held in trust by the state on behalf of the people. As the Michigan Department of Environmental Quality says, "The State, as the owner and trustee, has a perpetual responsibility to the public to manage these bottomlands and waters for the prevention of pollution, for the protection of the natural resources and to maintain the public's rights of hunting, fishing, navigation, commerce, etc. The State of Michigan's authority to protect the public's interest in the bottomlands and waters of the Great Lakes is based on both ownership and state regulation."[25]

Clay Township

Clay Township contains Harsens Island and the entire US portion of the delta. The South Channel is the passageway through the delta for large vessels, especially freighters. Dredging of the channel began in the late 1850s. In the early 1960s, dredging achieved a twenty-seven-foot depth, enough to allow passage by the largest cargo-bearing vessels.

More of Clay Township's jurisdiction—47 square miles—is water than island (35.5 square miles).[26] Water is a main identifier: a 1925-era, 136-foot steel-framed water tower still marks the landscape along M-29 near the north channel. Constructed to resemble a lighthouse, the tower was topped by a working navigation light until 1937.

Clay Township contains one of the largest remaining fragments of a globally imperiled ecosystem known as lake-plain prairie, low-lying, wet areas close to water. The fragment is adjacent to the three-thousand-acre St. John's Marsh, bordering on Lake St. Clair.

⌣

Before European settlement, the land area that is now Michigan contained 158,000 acres of lake-plain prairie, with over 80 percent occurring in Monroe, Wayne, and St. Clair counties. Only 745 acres, or 0.47 percent, of

When Drinking Water Killed

Not long after the United States and Canada formed a joint commission in 1909 to prevent and resolve disputes over boundary waters shared by the two nations, their governments asked the panel to investigate and report on the severity of pollution affecting those waters. The International Joint Commission's 1918 final report minced no words, calling the situation "generally chaotic, everywhere perilous, and in some cases disgraceful."* The peril included death from consuming public drinking water. The cause of the danger was a violation of common sense: cities were taking their drinking water from the same rivers in which upstream communities dumped their poorly treated or untreated sewage.

Among the boundary waters studied were the St. Clair and Detroit Rivers. The commission compiled health statistics from communities relying on the two waterways for drinking water, including Port Huron, St. Clair, Marine City, Algonac, Detroit, River Rouge, Ecorse, Wyandotte, and Trenton. The results were striking: typhoid fever death rates were highest in cities whose community water supplies were drawn from the foulest water. The St. Clair River was too polluted for drinking without extensive treatment for thirty-four miles south of Port Huron. Even worse was the Detroit River. "From Fighting Island to the mouth of the river the water is grossly polluted and totally unfit as a source of water supply. . . . Unfortunately, Wyandotte, Trenton and Amherstburg are taking their water supplies from this part of the river," the commission said.

Later in the report, the commission drew the link to public health. "The grossly polluted condition of boundary waters is doubtless the cause of the abnormal prevalence of typhoid fever throughout the territory bordering thereon." Those on land weren't the only victims. In 1907, a steamer traveling the Great Lakes pulled drinking water from the Detroit River, resulting in seventy-seven cases of typhoid fever. In 1913, on three

Great Lakes vessels carrying 750 people, there were three hundred cases of diarrhea, fifty-two cases of typhoid, and seven deaths.

Along the Detroit River, typhoid death rates rose south of the city of Detroit. In 1913 the rate was 29 per 100,000 in Detroit but 243 per 100,000 in Trenton. Detroit responded by chlorinating its water supply in 1916.

The commission observed that the death rates had declined in subsequent years and credited the investigation itself, saying that it had brought attention to the problem and led to greater use of bleaching powder and chlorine to disinfect drinking water. Still, "Violent outbreaks of typhoid fever have occurred, and the potential danger must continue to exist in view of the extensive pollution of these waters and the limitations and inefficient operation of water purification plants." The commission recommended that no untreated sewage be dumped into boundary waters and that standards be set to assure sanitary conditions. It called for modern sewage works in Detroit to control bacterial pollution. The consulting engineer for the City of Detroit said an adequate city sewage plant could be built for $8 million, the cost justifiable in light of public health and economic benefits. Instead, an epidemic of gastroenteritis erupted in 1926, affecting forty-five thousand people. In 1932, the city responded by moving its water supply intake from the near shore to the far side of Belle Isle along the shipping channel. In 1940 a primary wastewater treatment facility opened.

Growing awareness of the preventable mortality resulting from sewage-polluted drinking water promoted sewage treatment and especially chlorination of drinking water supplies. While saving precious lives, the chlorination solution reduced the sense of urgency about the aesthetic, recreational, and ecological impacts of contaminated lakes and rivers. It would be another fifty years before society would be ready to attack that problem head-on. In 1968, Michigan voters approved $335 million in bonds to build treatment plants that would once and for all dramatically reduce sewage pollution.

*International Joint Commission, "Final Report on the Pollution of Boundary Waters Reference," September 10, 1918, https://archive.org.

the prairie remains. Lake-plain prairies are rich with plant life. St. John's Wet Prairie Natural Area harbors over 160 species, including exquisite wildflowers such as blazing star and tall sunflower, and grasses such as big bluestem and Indian grass.

The larger St. Johns Marsh offers wildlife refuge zones as well as hunting zones. But it, too, is imperiled—by the invasive phragmites, a plant. Phragmites can grow up to twenty feet tall and crowd out native species, reducing biological diversity. Phragmites blocks shoreline views, is undesirable to most wildlife, and reduces water access. Demonstrating the significance of the threat, Clay Township has established a Phragmites Management Advisory Board.[27]

A host of project partners in 2016 were carrying on an aggressive marsh restoration project in the marsh, using aerial and on-the-ground herbicide applications and controlled burns. The collaborative included the Michigan Department of Natural Resources, the Huron-Clinton Metropolitan Authority, Harrison Township, the Michigan Chapter of Ducks Unlimited, Michigan Sea Grant, and the Southeast Michigan Council of Governments.

CHAPTER 3

Metropolis Bound

Water is of major importance to all living things; in some organisms, up to 90% of their body weight comes from water. Up to 60% of the human adult body is water. . . . the brain and heart are composed of 73% water, and the lungs are about 83% water. The skin contains 64% water, muscles and kidneys are 79%, and even the bones are watery: 31%.

—US Geological Survey, Water Science School

ake St. Clair has been called the heart of the Lakes. Some have tried to elevate it further, proclaiming it the sixth Great Lake. European explorers—and aboriginal peoples long before them—found five undisputedly great lakes. But is there a sixth? One could argue in favor of Ontario's Lake Nipigon to the northwest, and a member of Congress authored a short-lived law declaring Lake Champlain to the east to be number six. But a lake in the middle of them all has the strongest claim.

Volume of water is not the source of the argument. Lake St. Clair's one cubic mile is puny when compared to the 116 cubic miles of water in Lake

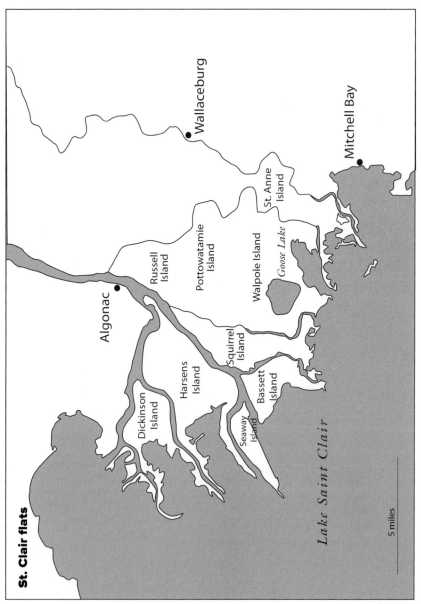

St. Clair flats

Wallaceburg

Mitchell Bay

St. Anne Island

Russell Island

Pottowatamie Island

Walpole Island

Goose Lake

Algonac

Squirrel Island

Harsens Island

Bassett Island

Dickinson Island

Seaway Island

Lake Saint Clair

5 miles

ELLEN WHITE

Erie, the smallest of the conventional five Great Lakes—or the 2,900 cubic miles of water in Lake Superior.[1]

Depth is not the source of the argument. Superior's deepest point is 1,333 feet below the water surface, Erie's 210. St. Clair's natural depth is never greater than 21 feet—it is so shallow, in fact, that continuous dredging is needed to increase the depth in the shipping channel to 27 feet and maintain this critical pathway of commerce.

Retention time is not the source of the argument. St. Clair completely turns over approximately every seven days. Erie takes 2.6 years and Superior 191 years.

Shoreline length is not the source of the argument. The shores of Superior span 2,726 miles, Erie 871 miles, and St. Clair 257 miles.

No, the argument for Lake St. Clair as the sixth Great Lake is rooted chiefly in one characteristic—location. It is the indispensable lake, the one that must be traversed to pass between the upper and lower lakes. If it did not exist, billions of dollars in engineering and construction costs would be necessary to break a route from sea to inland ports.

Lake St. Clair is more than a connector, however. Emptying into the Detroit River just miles northeast of downtown Detroit and Windsor, it is also close to large urban populations. Its fish stocks attract anglers. Its open waters attract boaters.

If a fishery is a measure of greatness, Lake St. Clair meets the standard. One fishing source identifies the lake as being responsible for nearly 30 percent of the sport fishing catch and 50 percent of all sport fishing that takes place in the Great Lakes.[2] "It has, over the years, gained a new respect amongst the 'world's' anglers, making it the 'little lake that could.'" It's especially famous for its muskie, or muskellunge, fishing. About 30 percent of charter fishing trips on the lake target muskie. Other species coveted by anglers that are in abundance in Lake St. Clair include yellow perch, walleye, and smallmouth bass. Michigan State University Extension calls the Lake St. Clair fishery "very intense," with more than twenty-two angler hours per acre, followed by runner-up Lake Erie, with less than ten hours per acre.[3]

Smallmouth bass fishing can be especially bountiful. One charter operator comments, "Once the summer patterns have settled in, it is not uncommon to catch upwards of 40 to 60 bass in a four-hour period, with many days providing more action than that. On our charter operation, clients (2 to 4) are treated to non-stop action throughout their 6-hour trip. This 'gamest of all sportfish' gives them all they can handle."[4]

By one estimate, communities around Lake St. Clair enjoy an annual economic impact of $1.7 billion from the lake.

Like other water bodies in southeast Michigan and across the United States and Canada, St. Clair has suffered its share of pollution abuse. In 1970, the discovery of high levels of mercury led to a shutdown of the lake's commercial fishery. Governments required steep pollution reductions by the source of the mercury, the Dow Chemical Company's chlor-alkali plant in Sarnia, Ontario. But mercury persists in the environment for decades, and additional mercury enters the Great Lakes ecosystem after traveling through the air hundreds or thousands of miles, often originating from coal-fired power plants. Advisories recommending limited consumption of some species, by some sub-populations, remain in effect on Lake St. Clair to protect public health from mercury and other contaminants.

In 1994, a billion-gallon discharge of untreated sewage from an Oakland County drain, flowing down the Clinton River, closed Lake St. Clair beaches with *E. coli* contamination for much of the summer. Twenty years later, in 2014, a 2.1-billion-gallon overflow of partially treated sewage stirred public outrage.

A prominent crusader against pollution in the years following the 1994 spill was Doug Martz, who called himself a "sludge buster," arriving at public meetings in a scuffed-up Cadillac limousine fitted with a toilet and loudspeakers on the roof and waving a plunger.

⌣

Citizens have argued for an official designation of St. Clair as the sixth Great Lake. In 2002, Jim LaHood, who owned St. Clair Shore's Lakeshore Lanes, a bowling alley, applauded the idea.[5] "I've always considered Lake St. Clair the greatest of all the Great Lakes," he told a *Los Angeles Times* reporter. "I'd get up every morning and look out on the lake. Of course it's a Great Lake. It's not as big as the other Great Lakes, but you can't see to the other side. It sure doesn't feel like an inland lake."

Size alone doesn't determine what is or isn't a great lake, or a Great Lake. The human heart plays a role, too.

The lake's European settlement reaches back over 335 years. The official state marker for Lake St. Clair, erected in 1979, asserts: "French explorers discovered and named Lake Saint Clair on August 12, 1679." Accurate to a point, the text refers to La Salle's entry into the lake aboard the *Griffon* that summer day, the feast of Sainte Claire of Assisi. That wasn't the first French name; maps show it known by the English equivalents "Seawater Lake" and "The Kettle." An Ojibwa name for the lake was Waawiyaataan, or Curved Shores.

Anchor Bay

From the St. Clair Flats, the lake's shoreline arcs north and west before its inevitable turn south. Inside the arc is Anchor Bay.

The bay is likely the most distinctive geographic and nautical characteristic of the lake next to the flats. Its name dates at least to 1809. In that year, a government surveyor for the British Crown fashioned a map of the river and lake. Anchor Bay "is shown and named with the explanation that there was a bar at the end of the north channel in consequence of which loaded vessels were required to anchor and lighten," that is, unload cargo in a smaller boat.[6]

The first significant community on the arc is Fair Haven. The creek that provided a magnet for the first settlement, Rivière des Cygnes (Swan River), reaches almost to today's village of Richmond some ten miles inland. "Swan Creek Settlement" was the early nineteenth-century name for the métis community that predated statehood. An 1810 survey map portrays a large Chippewa reservation of nearly six thousand acres surrounding and west of this creek. The city of Anchorville westward along the shore took its name from the bay in 1876.

The French heritage runs deep. A small tributary, Marsac Creek, enters the bay between Anchorville and New Baltimore at Marsac Point. The name may originate with an early Detroit settler, Jean Baptiste Marsac, born at Detroit in August 1739. The Marsac name can be found in histories of Michigan pioneers.

Next is New Baltimore. It may not sound European, but it was Pierre Yax who first made a settlement here in 1796. There is a slight resemblance to the Maryland city, since both face a bay, and ships once carried passengers here for stays along the water at high-quality hotels. The Grand Pacific House at 51065 Washington opened in 1881 during the town's golden era. The Italianate hotel and saloon were built of bricks made locally at Streits's brickyard.

Running southward behind the community into the lake was a tributary known on early maps as L'a Saline. The Salt River was so named because of the salt found along its banks, a precious trading commodity in the eighteenth and early nineteenth centuries.

The French heritage wraps further around this end of the lake until it terminates at the Grosse Pointe communities. Included in the geographic markings are Goulette Point, Auvase Creek, and Belle Maer.

Harrison Township

At the end of the arc is Harrison Township, named by the Territorial Council in 1827 after the military leader who took Detroit back from the British in the War of 1812. William Henry Harrison had helped secure the Northwest Territory for the United States during the conflict with the Western Confederacy force of Native Americans.

The township has grown to a population of twenty-six thousand. One of its key amenities is Lake St. Clair Metropark, which bisects two bodies of water that derive their names from the Europeans, Campau Bay and L'anse Creuse Bay. The 770-acre park, which opened in 1950, is best known for its beach and boating. It also features a sixteen-hundred-foot boardwalk, nature trails, and wetlands. More than 230 species of birds have been observed in the park. The Metropark has three marinas and eight boat ramps providing access to Lake St. Clair. The park's Olympic-sized swimming pool is a backup when pollution closes the park's beach.

The township's military heritage continues with Selfridge Air National Guard Base. The base dates to 1916 when the Packard Motor Car Company acquired a large tract of land on Lake St. Clair at the urging of its president, who was leading the company to begin developing aircraft engines for the nascent industry. In the spring of 1917, the Mount Clemens Business Men's Association and Detroit business leaders began lobbying the federal government to locate a military airfield at the site, known as Joy Aviation Field, for the Packard CEO, Henry Joy. They believed it could serve as a training facility for US flyers now that the nation had entered World War I. Because of the proximity to the lake for practice bombing, Washington agreed and made the site one of only nine military airfields in the country.

Mount Clemens

Mount Clemens is several miles from the mouth of the Clinton River. The mount in this city's name is purely figurative. The original land grant of 1811 to Christian Clemens put the site on the map. Clemens came to Michigan in 1795 and three years later was engaged in surveying this part of the wilderness before moving his residence here to open a distillery. His house became a temporary home for those moving to the area. He platted the original village in 1818 and, according to his gravestone, "contributed generously to its early prosperity. Here he spent his life and here he died, August 25, 1844."

Prosperity came to Mount Clemens via water midway through the nineteenth century. In the Civil War era, a well was sunk to obtain brine for salt production. "Because of the high cost of separating the salt from the various other minerals and elements in the water," says the state historical marker, "this process proved unprofitable."

All was not lost. Dorr Kellogg, a local miller, "decided to bath[e] in the warm sulfurous water. Impressed with its therapeutic qualities, city businessmen were inspired to invest in a bathhouse."[7] Sufferers from blood poisoning, diabetes, rheumatism, and skin diseases, among others, soon flocked to Mount Clemens as the curative powers of the local water became renowned. By 1900 nine bathhouses and over thirty hotels operated in the town, and by 1911 it boasted seventy-eight hotels and eleven bathhouses. It was hailed as "The Great Health & Pleasure Resort of Michigan."

The last of those bathhouses to remain began construction in 1898. Opened the next year, the Saint Joseph Sanitarium and Bath House at 215 North Avenue featured electric lights, a library, parlors, steam heat, and a hydraulic elevator. It offered baths using the mineral water pumped from over a thousand feet underground. According to the *National Journal of Homeopathic Medicine*, "This institution eclipses anything yet attempted in the Bath City."

In 1900, the Sisters of Charity of Mount Saint Joseph set aside the third floor of the building for a fifty-bed hospital. A member of the order founded one of the first state-licensed nurse-training programs here. Saint Joseph's eventually became the major hospital between Detroit and Port Huron. Its stately Colonial Revival building designed by local architect Theopholus Van Damme still stands.

The Clinton River flows through downtown Mount Clemens. In 1838, a major public works project stirred the town when construction began on the "Clinton-Kalamazoo Canal." When the canal was finished, its boosters said, boats—and commerce—would easily move from southeastern Michigan via Lake St. Clair up the Clinton and into the canal to connect all the way to Lake Michigan. A national recession and difficulties in construction permanently halted the project. After five years, the canal had progressed to Rochester. There it stopped, forever. Economics and the emergence of rail transportation killed the canal.

Clinton River

The lower stretch of the Clinton River illustrates both the abuse and the recovery of southeast Michigan's waters.

Originally, this waterway was known as the "Nottawasippee" by the Native Americans and French. The river was renamed to honor DeWitt Clinton, the governor of New York who championed the Erie Canal project that opened up the settlement of Michigan via water.

The principal branch of the river rises from wetlands in Springfield Township in Oakland County, northwest of the city of Pontiac, named for the great Odawa chief. It is piped and concealed under downtown Pontiac, reemerging to the east. The north and middle branches rise in northern Macomb County and join the main branch in Clinton Charter Township. The main branch flows eighty-three miles to Lake St. Clair. The river watershed encompasses 760 square miles, where nearly a million and a half people in some sixty municipalities live.

The Clinton River has a troubled environmental past but a potential blue future. The river is one of the Great Lakes "areas of concern" designated by the US and Canadian governments. The Clinton's designation reflected problems ranging from fecal coliform bacteria associated with sewage to polychlorinated biphenyl (PCB) and toxic metal contamination. Now, after thirty years of effort, the contamination is slowly easing under the care of dedicated citizens and government action.

The river, from Lake Orion to its mouth at Lake St. Clair, has been designated in the Nationwide Rivers Inventory as one of more than thirty-four hundred free-flowing river segments in the United States believed to possess one or more "outstandingly remarkable" natural or cultural values judged to be of more than local or regional significance.

Lake St. Clair Metropark has paid the price for the river's problems. Because of combined sewer overflows during storms and ineffective anti-pollution measures, the park beach has periodically experienced closures caused by *E. coli* in the water.

Hundreds of millions of dollars have been spent to reduce the sewage overflows that pour into the Clinton River and thence to Lake St. Clair, making it unsafe at times for swimming. One conduit for these flows is the Red Run Drain, which flows from Madison Heights in Oakland County (where it's enclosed) through Warren and Sterling Heights within Macomb County. The drain flows to Freedom Hill County Park and into the Clinton River near Hayes and Metropolitan Parkway. In 2014, torrential August rains led Oakland County communities to dump an estimated 2.1 billion gallons of sewage into watercourses that conveyed much of the pollution to the lake. Most was partially treated, but 140 million gallons were raw sewage.

That's one reason why elimination of combined sewer overflows and sanitary sewer overflows is part of the Clinton River cleanup plan. The blueprint also calls for control of polluted runoff from land, Superfund waste site and contaminated sediments remediation, spill notification, habitat restoration, and elimination of illicit household sewage connections to storm sewers and failing septic systems.

In 2015, the US Environmental Protection Agency directed $20 million in federal funds for Clinton River rehabilitation to the City of Sterling Heights, Macomb County, the Huron-Clinton Metropolitan Authority, the City of Auburn Hills, and the Army Corps of Engineers. The biggest single sum, $6.3 million, was to be used to restore habitat in Partridge Creek Commons, McBride Drain, and the Clinton River Spillway, greening more than thirty-two thousand linear feet.

St. Clair Shores

The sense of metropolis, of land devoted almost wholly to supporting human beings, deepens as you travel south by southwest to this suburb.

Bordered by I-94 on the west, Base Line Road on the south, and 14 Mile Road on the north, St. Clair Shores stretches eight miles along Lake St. Clair. Many canals add to its waterfront. The area was inhabited by the French as early as 1710, when it was called L'anse Creuse, "Little Bay." Water transport gave the community its start; rail transportation gave it an easy connection both north and south. The Detroit, Lakeshore, and Mt. Clemens Railway, also known as the Shore Line, began interurban rail service in September 1898. The route followed Jefferson Avenue from Detroit through the Grosse Pointe communities and into St. Clair Shores, terminating in Mount Clemens. The interurban brought Detroiters to the St. Clair Shores area for summer outings until the 1920s, when autos gained supremacy over the rails. Both rail and, initially, autos supported a resort town made possible by Lake St. Clair. After World War II, the municipality grew rapidly into a bedroom community for commuters, as it remains.

Toxic PCBs from undetermined sources have contaminated two of the city's canals leading to Lake St. Clair since 2001. Residents from adjacent neighborhoods refrain from swimming or fishing there. In 2015, work crews removed vaults where the PCBs pool underneath the intersection at Bon Brae and Harper. The toxins then they find their way into an underground drain system that empties out in the canals several blocks away. EPA officials hoped the action would reduce the volume of contamination.

Grosse Pointe Communities

Large classical lakefront homes with yards that unfurl to the lake dominate the view along much of the lakeshore here. They once signaled that executives in the auto industry lived here.

Five municipalities villages make up the land between Lake St. Clair and I-94 south of Eight Mile Road: Grosse Pointe Park, Grosse Pointe, Grosse Pointe Farms, Grosse Pointe Shores, and Grosse Pointe Woods. French street names still pop up: Cadieux, Charlevoix Grand Marais, Notre Dame, St. Clair. The peace of these lanes is a contrast to an event that took place in this area, as told by a Michigan Historical Marker in Grosse Pointe Park at Lakepointe and Windmill Pointe Drive:

> Encouraged by a potential alliance with the English, the Fox Indians besieged Fort Pontchartrain, Detroit, in 1712. Repulsed by the French and their Huron and Ottawa Indian allies, the Fox retreated and entrenched themselves in this area known as Presque Isle. The French pursued and defeated the Fox in the only battle fought in the Grosse Pointes. More than a thousand Fox Indians were killed in a fierce five-day struggle. Soon afterward French settlers began to develop the Grosse Pointes.

Development has eradicated many of the early-day waterways in this locality. Although the mouth of the Milk River, once the home of Ottawa Indians and, later, French settlers, is in St. Clair Shores, it once flowed about two miles through Grosse Pointe Woods. This was important habitat. The Milk's tributary, the Girard, originated near Kelly Road in Harper Woods. Once connected to drains built by farmers, the water flowed from Harper Woods to Lake St. Clair. Fox Creek flowed in the opposite direction toward the lake.

In the late nineteenth century and early twentieth century these streams, creeks, drains, and rivers were dramatically altered by government drainage efforts intended to eliminate marshes and bogs and create land for settlement. This policy continued into the modern era, with massive sewer construction. Today, virtually all vestiges of the original waterways are erased. Settlement, and sediment, have conquered.

Another Michigan historical marker tells the tale on the south side of Lake Shore Drive just beyond the Edsel and Eleanor Ford House at the Milk River Bridge:

The strip of land at the mouth of the Milk River was named Point a Guignolet for a grape-link berry that the French fermented into brandy. It later became known as Gaukler Point. The 1702 map of Lac Sainte Claire, attributed to Detroit founder Antoine de la Mothe, Sieur de Cadillac, shows an Ottawa village near the Milk River. This is the earliest documented settlement at the point. As early as 1796 some thirty French families lived in the same vicinity. Well into the nineteenth century, the Milk River settlement was called L'Anse Creuse.

The Fords owned more than one house, but southeast Michigan was their home. The structure here became their final residence, no doubt thanks to its location on the shore of Lake St. Clair. The eighty-seven-acre estate was completed in 1927; the house was designed by Albert Kahn, the grounds by landscape architect Jens Jensen. The house's website explains Jensen's role:

> Known as the master of the naturalistic approach to landscaping, Jensen's design style combines woodlands, meadows and wetlands in such a natural way that guests are usually not conscious of any man-made design. Jensen was known for his use of native plants, the sense of vast open space, the play of light and shadow and the element of time and season's change. His approach to landscape architecture sought to engage all five human senses—the sight of many colors and shapes, the sound of water running, the smell of flowers in bloom, the taste of berries, and the feeling of being surrounded by nature.

Jensen sought to promote "a style of design that celebrated the native Midwestern landscape" and "enlighten others of the value of these vanishing resources." The lakefront enabled creation of a shorebird refuge, and he reconfigured the shore by creating a peninsula with protected harbor to create habitat for birds and animals.

The Grosse Pointes have long been attractive as the best home for

HCMA and the Emerald Arc

Arching from southern St. Clair through Oakland, Livingston, Washtenaw, and Monroe Counties is a feature dubbed the "Emerald Arc" by a local land conservancy. The little-known arc provides the headwaters for several of southeast Michigan's major river systems, including the Clinton, Rouge, Huron, and Raisin.

The arc is also a watershed divide that provided a shortcut for Native Americans and early Europeans seeking to avoid hundreds of miles of travel along the Lake Michigan and Lake Huron coasts. In 1790, Englishman Hugh Heward and seven French indentured servants paddled up the Huron from Lake Erie in search of the cross-peninsula route. Taking a little more than a month, they traced a route that involved portaging from the Huron into the Grand watershed in what is now southeastern Livingston County, and all the way across to its mouth in Lake Michigan at what is now Grand Haven.

The Huron-Clinton Metropolitan Authority (HCMA) has over the past three-fourths of a century developed one of the outstanding regional park systems in the country The HCMA is that rare public policy idea—one that anticipated a future need and addressed it rather than responding to a problem. A regional park district encompassing Wayne, Oakland, Macomb, Washtenaw, and Livingston counties, the HCMA was sanctioned by the Michigan Legislature in 1939 and was approved in 1940 by the residents of the five counties. Funding yielded by a small property tax levy became available in 1942.

The proponents of the HCMA observed that future metropolitan growth would develop sensitive areas while simultaneously increasing the need for recreation lands. The solution was to develop a system of parks along the Huron and Clinton Rivers that would make outdoor excursions convenient for urban and suburban residents. The timing was right: without action, the lands that became parks would have been subdivided and developed. The thirteen parks cover twenty-four thousand acres, attract nine million visitors annually, and stretch along the bow of the Emerald Arc. Three are in the Clinton's watershed, the others within the Huron's.

A possible future direction for the HCMA is partnership with the state of Michigan, the city of Detroit, and urban redevelopment organizations in developing public access and facilities along the Detroit riverfront and Belle Isle.

The Emerald Arc has become a central feature of a major, private, land conservation initiative. The Ann Arbor–based Legacy Land Conservancy has set a goal of protecting twenty-five thousand acres of the most important lands in Washtenaw and Jackson Counties along the Arc, extending from Pinckney State Recreation Area on the north to Hayes State Park on the south. The target area includes portions of the Huron, Raisin, Grand, and Kalamazoo River watersheds.

downtown business executives. Just a few minutes by auto from the center of Detroit, perched on the shore of Lake St. Clair, their beauty and proximity combine to make a highly attractive setting for the families of tycoons and CEOs.

Beginning in 2012, Macomb County sought to take advantage of its St. Clair shoreline asset, with its resources including hundreds of water-related businesses and nearly thirty-two miles of Lake St. Clair coastline and the Clinton River with its many tributaries.

The "Blue Economy" initiative included "developing sensible land and water planning programs and projects to create sustainable outcomes that continue to celebrate our freshwater assets and grow them in a manner that can be experienced for generations to come."[8] Among the groups collaborating on the program were the Nautical Mile Merchants Association; the Huron-Clinton Metropolitan Authority, a regional park system; and the Clinton River Watershed Council, whose mission is "protecting, enhancing and celebrating the Clinton River, its watershed and Lake St. Clair."

CHAPTER 4

The Heart of the Lakes

In many ways, the fate of the world's fresh water will be determined by Michigan's stewardship.

—*The Waters of Michigan*

Where Lake St. Clair pours its water into the Detroit River begins an aquatic corridor of singular history and ecological value. Flowing southwest and then south, the Detroit River spans time and two great and friendly democracies. Once a highway for Native Americans and early European explorers, it became a critical front in a great war, a conduit for pioneers settling a new nation, the mixing place of human colors and cultures, a working river, the witness to some of the most intense industrialization on the planet, an environmental disgrace, and an early sentinel of urban and conservation recovery.

One piece of evidence for recovery: the Detroit River was the first in North America to receive a joint "Heritage River" designation from the

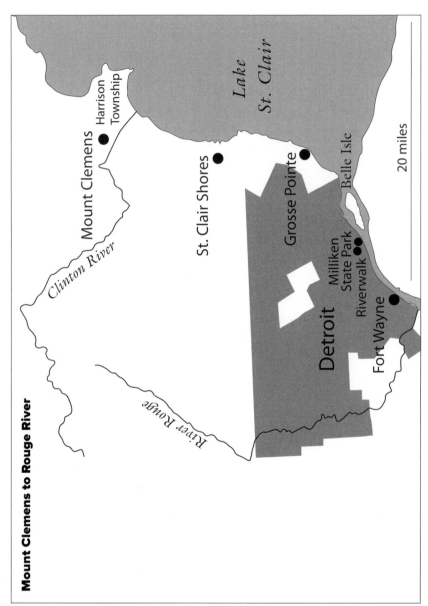

Mount Clemens to Rouge River

Harrison Township

Mount Clemens

Clinton River

Lake St. Clair

St. Clair Shores

Grosse Pointe

Belle Isle

River Rouge

Detroit

Milliken State Park

Riverwalk

Fort Wayne

20 miles

ELLEN WHITE

governments of the United States and Canada. Established in 1997, the Heritage River program designates a limited number of American rivers for their historic, economic and cultural importance. The first set of American Heritage Rivers, announced in July 1998, included such storied waterways as the Hudson, the Potomac, the Mississippi—and the Detroit River.

The thirty-two-mile river (actually a strait) would not have been a fit candidate for a Heritage River designation fifty years before. Municipalities and industries treated the river as a toilet. When thousands of ducks died from oil pollution on the river in the winter of 1948, sportsmen brought their carcasses to Lansing and dumped them on the walkway to the Capitol. Sewage and industrial chemicals fouled the river until the early 1970s, when tougher water pollution laws kicked in. By the early 1980s the river was measurably and visibly cleaner. But because legacy contamination persisted, in 1985 the Detroit River joined the list of Great Lakes areas of concern designated by the US and Canadian governments. Efforts on both sides of the border have restored two of eleven impaired uses, restrictions on drinking water and tainting of fish and wildlife flavor. The restoration of the remaining uses is expected to accelerate.

John Hartig, the first full-time manager at the Detroit River International Wildlife Refuge, in 2014 noted the significant fishery benefits of improved water quality: "In 2001, lake sturgeon reproduction was documented in the Detroit River for the first time in thirty years. In 2006, lake whitefish reproduction was documented in the river for the first time since 1916. During the 1970s, the walleye population was considered in 'crisis' and today, along with Lake Erie, the Detroit River is considered part of the 'Walleye Capital of the World.'"[1]

Cleanup had downstream benefits. Municipal sewage plant phosphorus controls and limitations on phosphorus in laundry detergent promulgated by Michigan in 1977 reduced discharges of the pollutant from Detroit's wastewater plant by 90 percent, sharply reducing algae blooms in Lake Erie. The return of Erie's blooms in the 2000s was thought to be primarily from other causes.

The Detroit Heritage River Water Trail is a vision made possible by a cleaner river. The plan for this pathway identifies corridors along the Detroit, Huron, Rouge, and Raisin Rivers suitable for recreational water trails—"blueways"—for canoeing and kayaking and associated improvements. The trail would begin at Maheras Gentry Park at 12550 Avondale, just beyond the tip of Belle Isle, and run to the village of Luna Pier at Lake Erie.

Geographically, Detroit is situated at the center of the Great Lakes system—and so much else. It is the oldest major city in the Midwest.[2] In the early 1820s, Schoolcraft described Detroit's beauty and strategic importance:

> A cursory examination of the map of the United States, will indicate its importance as a place of business, and a military depot. Situated on the great chain of lakes, connected, as they are, at almost innumerable points, with the waters of the Mississippi, the Ohio, the St. Lawrence, the Hudson, and the Red River of the North, it communicates with the ocean, at four of the most important points in the whole continent. And when these natural channels of communication shall be improved, so as to render them alike passable at all seasons of the year, the increasing products of its commerce and agriculture, will be presented with a choice of markets, at New-Orleans, New-York, or Montreal, an advantage derived from its singular position on the summit level in which the most considerable rivers, lakes, and streams in America, originate.[3]

Detroit is older than New Orleans, older than Chicago, older than Los Angeles. Located on the river, the church of St. Anne de Detroit has been an element of that history from the beginning. The congregation has continuously worshiped—in revised and larger buildings—since July 1701 when the first French settlers put down roots.[4] As Michigan's oldest parish, it has seen its share of difficulties. The first structure burned in 1703, the second in 1714. The congregation finally secured its house of worship when the present Gothic revival structure was built in 1887. One of the parish priests was

Last Stop on the Railroad

In the mid-nineteenth century, the torch of liberty burned brightly along the Detroit River. Black and white residents of the area collaborated in "communities of rescuers" to provide a haven for those escaping slavery. Situated less than one mile from freedom in Canada for the escaped slaves of the southern states, Detroit was the terminus of lines of the Underground Railroad from the 1820s until 1865. Thus the Detroit River, the passage to liberty, was nicknamed Jordan, in reference to the biblical stream that led to the Promised Land.

The Railroad was in fact a secret support network for escaping slaves. Often traveling on foot at night, they were housed by sympathizers before moving on. Several paths led slaves from various points in Michigan to the Canadian shore. A significant percentage of the approximately thirty thousand slaves who "rode" the Railroad to freedom passed through Detroit to reach Windsor.

African Americans were frequently the railroad's conductors and organizers, including Detroit's George DeBaptiste. Born in Virginia, he moved to Indiana before being forced to leave because of his antislavery activities in the Underground Railroad. He came to Detroit in 1846 because it had an established free black community and was the Railroad terminus. He owned a barbershop and a bakery in the city. In 1850, the same year the Fugitive Slave Act increased the exodus of slaves to Canada, DeBaptiste purchased the steamship *T. Whitney* and hired a white man to pilot it. Ostensibly a commercial vessel, the *Whitney* also secretly transported African Americans to Canada.

Twin sculpture memorials honor both ends of the final path to freedom in Detroit and Windsor. Located in Hart Plaza, the Detroit sculpture portrays nine slaves and a railroad conductor gazing at Canada as they await a boat to cross the river. The Windsor sculpture, on River Front

Drive, includes a tower symbolizing the Eternal Flame of Freedom. A former female slave holds a baby while a former male slave gives thanks. A Canadian conductor welcomes them.

Kimberly Simmons, historian, executive director, and president of the nonprofit Detroit Project, has pursued designation of the Detroit River as a United Nations Educational, Scientific and Cultural Organization (UNESCO) World Heritage Site for years. The river's role as an escape route to freedom deserves recognition on a global scale, she says.[*] "It's a natural border shared by two countries and drove up to 25,000 people to come here to find freedom." There were 1,052 sites in the world in late 2016, but only 18 in Canada and only 23 in the United States. Given such rare status in the two nations, a UNESCO designation of the Detroit River could have economic value, Simmons said. "Our river has the opportunity, not to just draw people to see a pretty river, but to draw big tourism dollars." To be included on the World Heritage list, sites must be of outstanding universal value. Humanity's longing for liberty and self-determination is a universal value whose story is vividly told by the history of the Detroit River.

---

[*]CBC Radio News, "Kimberly Simmons Is Fighting to Make the Detroit River a UNESCO World Heritage Site," http://www.cbc.ca.

Reverend Gabriel Richard, cofounder of the Catholepistemiad of Michigania, which later became the University of Michigan. He also served as territorial representative in the US Congress.

The merchant trade in furs was the first great Detroit industry. The city's position on the water enabled it to become a center for maritime food production, housing the largest catcher and jobber of freshwater fish in North America. The S.H. Davis & Co. firm opened in Detroit in 1855, with offices at 42 West Water Street. When Samuel Davis sold his company in 1898, he continued to work in the business and, as president of the Wolverine Fish

Company, operated the second largest freshwater fish-handling operation in the country.[5]

Conflict is a theme running through the post-European settlement era of the region. East of what is now downtown Detroit, the "Battle of Bloody Run" marked the fiercest conflict of Chief Pontiac's uprising. In late July 1763, British and Indian forces clashed as Captain James Dalyell led about 260 soldiers across Parent's Creek. The Indians launched a surprise attack that devastated the British. Dalyell and some 60 of his men were killed.

A state historical marker in Brownstown Township tells of the 1812 battle between forces under Tecumseh and American troops. One in Trenton erected in 1962 previously portrayed a similar theme for the Battle of Monguagon. It was replaced in 2012 and features text speaking of "Native Americans" and "Michigan Wyandot." The 2013 marker for "Council Point/ Pontiac's Council" in Lincoln Park similarly speaks of the native name of its subject—Obwandiyag—and of the tribes' fight for their homeland and rights.

Labor history has also suffered neglect. Michigan was once a labor bastion, and Detroit was home to neighborhoods of thousands of union workers during the twentieth century. Collective bargaining agreements between auto workers and their employers helped raise the standard of living in southeast Michigan to new highs during the post–World War II years.

Not far from the Detroit River, the Fort Street Rouge River Bridge is a critical part of Michigan's labor history. On March 7, 1932, unemployed autoworkers, their families, and union organizers gathered at the bridge in frigid temperatures. They planned to march to the Ford Rouge Plant and present a list of demands to the Ford Motor Company. A confrontation with police resulted in the deaths of five marchers and the wounding of nineteen others.

The history of the Rouge reaches far into the past. It provided a gateway for aboriginal peoples to journey from the Detroit River for miles inland. The early settlers used it for the same purpose. Henry Ford realized its usefulness in fulfilling his vision for a mammoth manufacturing complex

The Rouge Recovery

On a summer day in 1985, a stocky man with a cockeyed grin and an Irish name towed a group of reporters, videographers, government officials, and advocates to a viewing point on a bridge over the Rouge River in Dearborn. He pointed downward. In the water, one member of the group spotted a staggeringly plentiful school of fish wiggling downstream. But then the scent reached his nostrils. He looked again. The dark objects in the light green waters weren't fish, but human feces. Like others in the group, he groaned his disgust. The Clean Water Act had taken effect thirteen years before, yet raw sewage was fouling this river?

The tour guide was Jim Murray, chair of state government's Water Resources Commission, and his purpose was to shock—and to propel action. Focusing attention on a southeast Michigan river abandoned to pollution, he hoped to generate outrage and cleanup.

Ignoring warnings, in his childhood Murray had played in the foul waters of a branch of the Rouge in what is now Westland. Now, approaching forty, he vowed to drive state and local governments, the public, and journalists to the cause of Rouge River recovery. In the next thirty years, Murray would realize much of his dream.* But it came only as a nightmare ended.

French explorers had purportedly named the Rouge for the red tint from the rushes on its banks. Over time, as early settlement was succeeded by resource exploitation, the name came to be associated with the reddish-brown color of its polluted waters, particularly toward its mouth at the Detroit River.

There, the massive, 1,100-acre Ford plant belched smoke and dumped massive amounts of untreated industrial waste and oil and grease into both rivers. For the rest of the century, the site harbored blast furnaces, steel mills, foundries, metal-stamping facilities, an engine plant, a glass-manufacturing plant, a tire plant, and a powerhouse. It was the Henry Ford system in full flower, but the flowers wilted under the weight of pollution. In fact, in 1969, the oil-matted river caught fire, erupting in flames and blackening the sky near the I-75 highway bridge.

But it wasn't industry alone that fouled the Rouge. The river suffered from being an urban waterway, with a significant proportion of the lands draining into it paved. The watershed today is more than 50 percent urbanized. Less than 25 percent remains undeveloped. Impermeable surfaces such as roads and parking lots funnel tainted stormwater into rivers and creeks rather than allowing it to filter into the ground slowly. The same phenomenon fosters flash flooding.

The four major branches of the Rouge (Main, Upper, Middle, and Lower) span 126 river miles. More than 1.35 million people in forty-eight municipalities and three counties (Oakland, Washtenaw, and Wayne) inhabit the watershed. All of them flush toilets. For years leading up to the late twentieth century, overwhelmed by storms, municipal treatment plants dumped a repulsive load of untreated or partially treated feces into branches of the Rouge. Most people shunned the river, and many didn't even know it snaked through their communities. It was a sewer.

But thanks in large part to Murray's skill with the news media, what some called his annoying persistence, and societal revulsion at the condition of the Rouge, the health of the river was about to change in the mid-1980s. The year 1985 was a turning point for the Rouge. Murray's Water Resources Commission set a goal of making the Rouge safe for swimming again by 2005. He led the media tour. And tragically that year, a thirty-one-year-old Novi man fell into the Rouge, swallowed some river water, and died two weeks later of leptospirosis, or "rat fever." Said Murray: "I think one of the reasons the pollution has been tolerated as long as it has is that we've not been able to pin more things like this on it directly."

In 1985, along with four other water bodies in the heart of lakes, the Rouge joined the list of Great Lakes "areas of concern," or pollution hotspots, determined by the United States and Canada to need concentrated cleanup. The river's combination of toxic chemical contamination and massive sewage pollution ranked it among the most degraded in the nation.

The area-of-concern designation came with limited federal funding but a structure for identifying the river's problems and developing a plan to correct them. Significant money came in 1992, when local US representative John Dingell won congressional approval of the Rouge River National Wet Weather Demonstration Program, which over two decades brought more than $350 million in federal funds to the watershed. A total of more than $1 billion has been spent on the river's cleanup. The vast majority of the money corrected sewage overflows, but substantial sums also supported stream bank stabilization, dam removal, and public education. Rouge communities cumulatively spent tens of millions more addressing sewage and stormwater pollution.

In 2011 the thirty-five-member Alliance of Rouge Communities reported "major progress" in the restoration of the Rouge River. Pollutant loads from combined sewage overflows had decreased by 90 to 100 percent during most storms and snowmelts. The majority of the waters in the Rouge River watershed met at least some state water quality standards. Fish and wildlife populations in the watershed were rebounding. The Rouge wasn't all the way back, but it was in recovery.

And the most notorious industrial symbol of the Rouge's degradation, the Ford plant, underwent reinvention. Under the direction of architect Bill McDonough and with the support of Ford Motor Company CEO William Ford Jr., sustainability became the organizing principle for the factory. The redesign overhauled storm water management using natural processes, including a "living roof." Manufacturing processes at the plant minimized waste. The Rouge plant features a Gold LEED Visitor Center, has a paint plant that captures fumes to create fuel cells, has plants treating decades of soil pollution, and is now home to wildlife.

The City of Detroit is also contributing to the Rouge comeback—while protecting its residents from foul sewage backups in their basements and saving hundreds of millions of dollars. The solution is "green infrastructure," techniques that soak up or slow stormwater before it can enter drains, overwhelm sewage plant capacity, and flow poorly treated or untreated into the Rouge.

It's green because the techniques include rain gardens and bioswales—vegetated strips that capture and filter pollutants in stormwater. It's also green because it beautifies communities, with other benefits including increased property values, reduced stormwater charges, and even lower crime rates.

Green infrastructure requires open land for the construction of rain gardens and wetlands. Detroit's city government controls approximately 40 percent of its land area, providing a unique opportunity to demonstrate the techniques' effectiveness. Fiscally, it's clearly effective; instead of spending $1.2 billion to construct a massive tunnel to capture polluted runoff, the city is spending $50 million on green infrastructure on its far west side, which has sent torrents of floodwater into the Rouge. Mayor Michael Duggan is firmly behind the initiative. "Detroit is going to be a national leader in using our vacant land in a way that is both beautiful and environmentally sensitive," the mayor said.

Wayne County is a partner in a singular effort to restore an urban watershed corridor, the Rouge River Gateway Ecosystem Restoration Project. Launched in 2001, the plan is designed to promote sustainable development in the recovering Rouge basin. In the first ten years, the project saw completion of the first phase of the Rouge Greenway, linking Wayne County's Hines Park to Henry Ford Community College, the

University of Michigan–Dearborn campus, the Henry Ford Estate, and the Michigan Avenue corridor.

In 2016, more than three decades after launching the Rouge River rescue, Murray was pleased. "The greatest story behind the Rouge project," Murray said, "is that after 30 years the public is engaged, the education community is involved at the elementary, secondary and college levels and the regulatory agencies and local government have entered a new era of collaboration, replacing the top down, throw money at the problem and 'Big Brother will save us syndrome.'"[†]

---

[*]David Runk, "Michigan's Rouge River Returns to Health," *Washington Post*, May 24, 2006.

[†]Personal communication with author, April 11, 2016.

that would take in raw materials and turn out a finished motor vehicle. Access to the river was essential for transportation; so, too, was clean and inexpensive water for manufacturing, available because of the supply found in the nearby fresh sources.

The life of the Rouge plant began in 1917, and within a decade Henry Ford transferred the assembly line from the Highland Park facility. It was the site where Ford Motor built World War I submarine chasers known as "Eagle" boats. It became in the mid-1920s the largest manufacturing center in the world. It also became a source of pollution that threatened the Detroit River.

Along the Rouge in Dearborn is a history park known until the 1990s as the Henry Ford Museum and Greenfield Village and now simply as the Henry Ford. Ford dedicated the site to his friend and fellow inventor Thomas Edison in 1929. The dedication coincided with the fiftieth anniversary of the invention of the incandescent light bulb. Originally called the Edison Institute, the museum was to showcase the artisan creations, tools, and innovations that had transformed American life. Ford put on display hundreds of thousands of objects from everyday life that had helped produce a high standard of living, and he fashioned an outdoor park full of historic buildings relocated and thus preserved from the wrecking ball of progress. Among them are the bicycle shop where the Wright brothers experimented with powered flight; the Menlo Park laboratory complex where Edison worked on his many inventions; structures associated with George Washington Carver and Luther Burbank, botanical geniuses; and one of the courthouses where Abraham Lincoln plied his trade as a circuit lawyer in rural Illinois and that helped form his passion for the American dream of equal opportunity and justice under law. Said Ford: "I am collecting the history of our people as written into things their hands made and used." "Education is the greatest force in civilization."[6]

A striking addition to the park was relocation of a southern plantation and slave quarters. Both are open to the visitor, yielding a deeper understanding of a prior way of life in part of America based on involuntary servitude. Greenfield Village had, as a major goal, education of Americans about their past. The opportunity exists, for the careful visitor, to understand all aspects of US history, both proud and squalid. Not far from the plantation and slave quarters is the Maddox home, also a Ford acquisition that shows how free blacks in the post–Civil War era were able to acquire land and build a homestead.

The Ford Museum continues this tradition with an exhibit, With Liberty and Justice for All, which profiles the antislavery movement, the woman's suffrage movement, and the civil rights movement. It harbors the Rosa Parks bus and George Washington's camp cot. Laura Tokie, assistant editor of the magazine *Curator*, lauded the exhibit: "This is our history, warts and all, and it is good to remember. But this is not only about remembering. The Henry Ford has created an experience that resonates with and extends history."[7]

The 727-foot high central tower of the Renaissance Center is a curious modern feature of downtown Detroit. Built in 1977 to help restore the city's fortunes after the tumult of the 1960s, it originally almost ignored the advantage of adjacent water. Added to bunker-like features on the Jefferson

The Southeast Michigan Shipbuilders

The shipbuilders along southeast Michigan waterways have played an important part in American history.

Marine City was the region's early shipbuilding capital but proved too far from the center of population and a suitable workforce. In the last decades of the nineteenth century, Detroit took command.*

Captain Stephen Kirby incorporated the Detroit Dry Dock Company in 1872, locating it at Atwater and Orleans Streets. In 1877 the company bought Wyandotte Shipbuilding. Detroit Dry Dock ran the two yards until 1922, producing a wide variety of vessels, from lake steamers to railroad ferries. Detroit Dry Dock and the Dry Dock Engine Works teamed up to build dozens of Great Lakes ships. In 1899 the two companies were consolidated into the Detroit Shipbuilding Company.* Workers built wooden vessels in shipyards along the Detroit River and repaired them by hand in the dry docks. Some memorable vessels turned out by the Detroit Dry Dock Company:

- Launched in 1892, the *Chicora* was 209 feet long. It was built for the Graham & Morton Transportation Company to carry passengers and cargo between Wisconsin and southern Michigan.
- The Detroit Shipbuilding Company's best-remembered ship is the *Columbia*, a steamship launched in 1902 that carried passengers from downtown Detroit to the amusement park on Boblo Island until 1991.
- On April 20, 1895, the *Argo*, the last large commercial wooden vessel built along the Detroit River, was launched. After that, the Detroit Dry Dock Company used only steel hulls made at the Wyandotte yard it had purchased in 1879.

After World War I began, the Detroit Shipbuilding Company began manufacturing ships for the European nations here and at its shipyards in Wyandotte. When the United States entered the war in 1917, it began building "Lakers" to US government specifications.

In 1923 the Detroit and Cleveland Navigation Company paid the Detroit Shipbuilding Company $2.5 million in cash to build the largest pure side-wheel steamships ever constructed—the *Greater Detroit* and the *Greater Buffalo*.[‡] The "Frog Line" boats ran from the time the frogs came out of hibernation until they burrowed back in for the winter.

Large vessels were not the only nautical products manufactured in Detroit. "More than any other single place in the country, the foot of Motor Boat Lane in Detroit became the influential development center for powerboating in the period between about 1905 and 1915." Along the riverfront east of the Indian Village neighborhood, near the famed Pewabic Pottery and across from Belle Isle, this district housed several firms that "drew from an unusual talent pool of boat builders, naval architects, and engine designers sharing their knowledge to create some of the fastest and most powerful motor craft in the world, ranging from speedboats to cruisers." A leading twentieth-century marine architect, John L. Hacker, got his start by becoming "fascinated by what he found on Detroit's waterfront."[§]

By designing and manufacturing wooden small craft and small steel fighting ships, American Cruiser Company, Chris-Craft Corporation, Fisher Boat Works of Detroit, Gar Wood Industries, and the Hacker Boat Company all contributed to the ultimate Allied victory in World War II. Some produced patrol torpedo vessels, the boat made iconic by the story of future president John F. Kennedy. And "without landing craft from Michigan, the invasions of Europe and the Pacific islands would have been long delayed, if not impossible." A Chris-Craft landing craft was first ashore on D-Day.[*]

The keel for this craft had been laid during World War I. Though it secured a minor portion of the military contracts for boat construction, two of the region's major steel shipyards, Detroit Shipbuilding Company and Great Lakes Engineering Works, aided in building cargo ships to carry armaments and other war materiel across the Atlantic. Smaller firms produced lifeboats and workboats that aided the war effort.[††]

That marine matters have been central to Detroit should be no surprise. By the 1840s, three steamships a day were arriving at the town waterfront, bringing hundreds of settlers. One of the city's iconic sites is Mariners' Church. The Gothic Revival building was erected in 1849 at Woodward Avenue and Woodbridge Street. The cathedral has been devoted to serving the spiritual needs of Great Lakes ship crews for nearly 170 years. In 1955, the structure was relocated to a spot adjacent to the Detroit-Windsor tunnel entrance to enable construction of a new, modern Civic Center Plaza. Gordon Lightfoot's 1975 ballad "The Wreck of the Edmund Fitzgerald" gave it popular culture immortality as the shrine where "the church bell chimed 'til it rang twenty-nine times": "In a musty old hall in Detroit they prayed, / in the "Maritime Sailors' Cathedral."

*Detroit Historical Society, Encyclopedia of Detroit, "Detroit Drydock Company," https://detroithistorical.org.

†Historic American Engineering Record: Dry Dock Engine Works, HAER no. MI-330, https://cdn2.hubspot.net/hubfs/133291/images/MG%202017%20Website/pdfDownloads/bibliography/Dry_Dock_Engine_Works.pdf?t=1499788417005.

‡Great Lakes Maritime Institute, "The *S.S. Greater Detroit* 1924–1950—the Flagship of the Detroit & Cleveland Navigation Company," http://www.glmi.org/greater%20detroit%20history%20%20b.pdf.

§Scott M. Peters, *Making Waves: Michigan's Boat-Building Industry, 1865–2000* (Ann Arbor: University of Michigan Press, 2015), 66–67.

**Ibid., 149ff.

††Ibid., 88–90.

Avenue side, the seven-tower complex appeared to turn its face not to the water or the city but inward, where visitors were often lost in a maze of walkways and changing elevations that made navigating the fifteen-acre site a challenge.

In 1996 the RenCen was acquired by General Motors Corporation for relocation of its world headquarters. Ever since, the auto company has worked on rectifying the design mistakes and oversights, building a winter garden on the water side to open up to the RiverWalk, emphasizing the natural feature that is just steps away. A hotel remains at the core of the development, rising taller than any other structure in Michigan.

Near the RenCen, Michigan's first state park in the middle of a city capitalizes on the beauty of the Detroit River. The thirty-one-acre William G. Milliken State Park and Harbor is designed to bring visitors physically and emotionally closer to the city's original and still most precious asset. Formerly Tricentennial State Park and Harbor, it was renamed and dedicated in 2009.

At the site of a former shipbuilding facility and dry dock in the park, later repurposed as a warehouse for the Globe Trading Company, the Department of Natural Resources Outdoor Adventure Center seeks to bring Michigan's outdoors into the heart of its city. Visitors engage in hands-on activities, explore exhibits, and enjoy simulations, passing through the canopy of a massive bur oak tree, walking across a suspension bridge, stepping into a fishing boat, and seeing fish native to Michigan in a giant aquarium. The renovated building was born in the late 1860s as the Dry Dock Engine Works, where young Henry Ford worked as an apprentice. Like many premodern structures, it was abandoned, left to deteriorate, and sat vacant.

Adjacent to the Dequindre Cut, an urban greenway occupying a former railroad bed, the Adventure Center sits at its intersection with the Detroit RiverWalk. When complete, this pathway will link with the Iron Belle Trail, a statewide hiking and biking route that travels northeast along the Detroit River, taking in portions of Milliken State Park and running by the Center. The planned route also points in the opposite direction, taking one southwest along the RiverWalk to Rosa Parks Boulevard, through Mexicantown, across

Milliken and Detroit

It might seem odd that Michigan's first urban state park, in heavily Democratic Detroit, is named after a patrician Republican governor from the northern part of the state. But the park's namesake, the state's longest-serving governor, William G. Milliken, had a view of Detroit different from most members of his own party. "Cities have always been the center of civilization as we have known it. We are now at the point where we will determine whether our cities become monuments—or death mounds—of our civilization," Milliken said in a 1977 address to fellow governors. "If we can't solve our urban problems, we can't solve the problems of America."*

Milliken did more than talk about Detroit. In an unlikely partnership with the earthy Democratic mayor of the city, Coleman Young, he fashioned a state aid package for Detroit that generated an annual fight among legislators. Milliken and allies won, narrowly, each time.

"Detroit had become a code word for black, and in turn my name had become a code word for Detroit," Young said. "It was not politically expedient for Milliken to work closely with me, but he had enough integrity to screw the politics and get on with what was right and necessary."

Milliken's commitment to urban policy was also illustrated by the opening of an urban affairs office in Detroit and efforts—ultimately unsuccessful—to connect the city and suburbs with a light rail system.

Late into life, Milliken adhered to his belief in the revitalization of Detroit and other urban centers in the state. He praised Rick Snyder, the Republican governor in 2011: "He recognizes that we are one state . . . and the problems of Detroit and other cities in Michigan require the attention of us all."

---

*Dave Dempsey, *William G. Milliken: Michigan's Passionate Moderate* (Ann Arbor: University of Michigan Press, 2006), 125.

The Detroit River was the final stretch of the Underground Railroad to freedom for many African Americans fleeing slavery prior to the Civil War. Businessman George DeBaptiste purchased the steamship *T. Whitney* and hired a white man to pilot it. Ostensibly a commercial vessel, the *Whitney* also secretly transported African Americans to Canada.

Paddlers passing beneath the Blue Water Bridge that links Port Huron and Sarnia are at an aquatic trailhead. The Blueways of St. Clair offers sixteen routes. Paddlers choosing the Blue Water Bridges Excursion are encouraged to put in where they choose upstream of the Blue Water Bridges, where lake ends and river begins. COURTESY OF THE BLUEWAYS OF ST. CLAIR.

The Detroit River International Underground Railroad Memorial Monument consists of sculptures in Detroit and Windsor, Ontario, commemorating the route to freedom for escaping slaves across the river prior to the Civil War. This is the Detroit sculpture, *Gateway to Freedom*, which shows six fugitive slaves preparing to board a boat to cross to Canada. George DeBaptiste, a Detroit leader in the antislavery movement, points to freedom. The monument in Windsor, *Tower of Freedom*, features a former slave raising his arms to celebrate his emancipation. A Quaker woman offers assistance to a woman and her child, while another child looks back toward Detroit.

COURTESY OF THE DETROIT RIVERFRONT CONSERVANCY.

Former US representative John Dingell and his wife and successor in office, Representative Deborah Dingell. John Dingell was architect of the federal law creating the Detroit River International Wildlife Refuge, which has become a focal point for environmental education and the river's natural renaissance.

This Detroit River scene between 1900 and 1915 documents the river's intense commercial and recreational uses. Under the water's surface, though, rode pollutants that caused outbreaks of lethal cholera until chlorination finally protected drinking water in the 1920s.

In the late 1800s, the White Star line launched the *Tashmoo*, built at the Wyandotte shipyards, to ferry passengers between Detroit and Port Huron. Later the vessel made trips on a downriver swing that included Sugar Island and Lake Erie.

This 1905 view of the St. Clair River from Port Huron's Pine Grove Park shows the timeless lure of these waters and the timeless passage of commercial ships from the lower to the upper Great Lakes.

The St. Clair Flats has long been a waterfowler's and angler's paradise. Organized as the St. Clair Fishing and Shooting Club of Detroit in 1872, what became The Old Club in 1902, began with twenty-six boathouses and a clubhouse on stilts. By 1890 sportsmen could depart from the foot of Woodward Avenue in Detroit for a mere one-hour boat trip to the club.

"Ice yachters" gathered for an outing on Lake St. Clair in 1900.

As this 1901 image of freighters passing Detroit Light testifies, the Detroit River had become an indispensable artery for American commerce, ultimately connecting the grain and iron producers of the Midwest with eastern consumers. Early in the twenty-first century, shipping, freight/commercial traffic, and warehousing contributed over sixty-five thousand Michigan jobs and $3.3 billion in annual wages.

Downstream of the Detroit River, Michigan's Lake Erie waters have suffered from on-and-off algae blooms since the early 2000s. Governments and citizens are working to reduce phosphorus pollution from farms and urban streets that fuels the algae. COURTESY OF JANINE MIDDLESWORTH.

John Hartig, manager of the Detroit River International Wildlife Refuge for over fourteen years. He was also a community leader in articulating the economic benefits accruing from environmental cleanup and the author of *Burning Rivers*, documenting the change from the use of Great Lakes waters as waste receptacles to amenities. "We've seen a substantial improvement in water quality, an amazing ecological revival, and the return of bald eagles and peregrine falcons and ospreys and lake sturgeon and whitefish and walleyes and mayflies. It just goes on and on," he said. COURTESY OF THE US FISH AND WILDLIFE SERVICE.

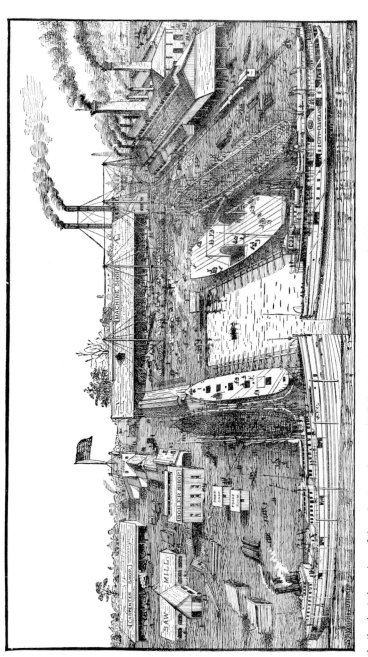

In the last decades of the nineteenth century, Detroit took command of Great Lakes shipbuilding. The Detroit Dry Dock Company was incorporated in 1872, located at Atwater and Orleans Street. In 1877 the company bought Wyandotte Shipbuilding. Detroit Dry Dock ran the two yards until 1922, producing a wide variety of vessels, from lake steamers to railroad ferries. Detroit Dry Dock and the Dry Dock Engine Works teamed up to build dozens of Great Lakes ships.

The Detroit riverfront was once primarily industry territory. Railroads terminated there. Silos and warehouses dominated. Now it is a lure for exercisers, anglers, water lovers, and those looking close to home for an escape from the stresses of everyday life.

In the heart of the city, the Detroit RiverWalk provides a chance for a new generation to learn how to fish. Despite legacy contamination from decades ago, the river's fish are safe to eat, following state health guidelines.

The massive Ford Rouge complex became in the mid-1920s the largest manufacturing center in the world. It also became a source of pollution that threatened
the Detroit River. Under the direction of architect Bill McDonough and with the
support of Ford Motor Company CEO William Ford Jr., sustainability became the
organizing principle for the factory. USED WITH PERMISSION OF THE DETROIT PUBLIC LIBRARY DIGITAL COLLECTIONS.

After a local miller bathed in the warm, sulfurous well water at Mt. Clemens in the
late 1800s and declared it therapeutic, a new business line arose. Sufferers from
blood poisoning, diabetes, rheumatism, and skin diseases, among others, soon
flocked to the city. By 1900 nine bathhouses and over thirty hotels operated in the
town, and by 1911 it boasted seventy-eight hotels and eleven bathhouses. It was
hailed as "The Great Health & Pleasure Resort of Michigan."

This National Oceanic and Atmospheric Administration satellite view displays the entire corridor from Port Huron to Lake Erie. Plumes of lighter color are sediment runoff.

In the 1940s and 1950s, lax pollution laws and poor stewardship led to fouled rivers throughout southeast Michigan, killing off fish and discouraging recreation. As late as 1984, the death of a canoeist exposed to pathogens in the Rouge River at last gave impetus to cleanup. COURTESY OF THE BENTLEY HISTORICAL LIBRARY, UNIVERSITY OF MICHIGAN.

The Detroit wastewater treatment facility was one of the largest in the world for decades. Its discharge clogged the Detroit River with sewage and tainted it with chemicals. In the 1960s and 1970s, massive new controls and federal and state laws led to a steep decline in phosphorus concentrations and discharges from the plant, fueling the river's recovery. COURTESY OF THE BENTLEY LIBRARY.

A globally imperiled ecosystem known as lake-plain prairie sits adjacent to the 3,000-acre St. John's Marsh, bordering on Lake St. Clair. Before European settlement, the land area that is now Michigan contained 158,000 acres of lake-plain prairie, with over 80 percent occurring in Monroe, Wayne, and St. Clair Counties. Less than 1% of the prairie remains. St. John's Wet Prairie Natural Area harbors over 160 species, including exquisite wildflowers such as blazing star and tall sunflower, and grasses such as big blue stem and Indian grass.
COURTESY OF TODD MARSEE, MICHIGAN SEA GRANT.

THIS MEMORIAL IS DEDICATED
IN THE MEMORY OF:

MANUEL ABASTA   ROMUALDO ALVAREZ
JAMES BEESLEY   ROSWELL BROWN
KEITH VERNER   GERALD CURTIS
WALTER WOODS   CHARLES EPPERSON
DONALD FOGAL   DONALD WILLIAMS
KENNETH HAWES   VERNERD WOOLSTENHULME
FRANK POLK   JAMES REIGHARD
GARY ROEHM   CLAYBOURNE SIMPKINS
GLEN VERNER   GUILLERMO TARAN
DONALD HARDEL   RAYMOND COMEAU
MARTIN LARETZ   PATRICK DINGMAN

This monument in Fort Gratiot County Park, just north of Port
Huron, commemorates the twenty-two workers who lost their lives
in an explosion during construction of a new water intake for the Detroit water
system in December 1971. The project excavated more than one billion pounds of
rock. The expansion pumped clean water into an eighty-two-mile system of water
mains supplying Detroit and Flint. COURTESY OF THE SCULPTOR, PAULA SLATER (HTTPS://PAULASLATER.COM).

In 2012 the River Raisin Legacy Project commenced a comprehensive initiative to restore the environment that will produce a vibrant and balanced ecosystem for the region. Fishing, wildlife viewing, kayaking, and trail hiking are featured. With removal of low-head dams, customized rock arch ramps built facing downstream, and bypass channels, kayaks and canoes can traverse twenty-three miles of the river from Dundee, Michigan, to Lake Erie. Kayaks can be seen on the River Raisin almost daily from the spring through the fall.

The River Raisin has a rich history to contemplate, from its critical role in the lives of indigenous peoples, to the War of 1812 battle, to industrial development, to today's environmental recovery. The community is capitalizing on the river as an amenity instead of treating it as a receptacle for waste or as an afterthought.

the historic Fort Street Bridge, and then traversing River Rouge, Ecorse, and downriver communities alongside the west channel of the Detroit River as it splits at Grosse Ile until veering off in Gibraltar to head west toward Ann Arbor.[8]

The RiverWalk was a breakthrough in reuniting people with the strait in the Detroit and promoting its aesthetics and recreational uses. The strong support of General Motors, the Kresge Foundation, the Community Foundation for Southeast Michigan, and all the other donors to the new RiverWalk Conservancy made this possible. Opened to the public in June 2007, the generally sixty-foot-wide path has separate lanes for pedestrian and bicycle traffic. Running directly along the river, the route offers scenic views of these waters, passing freighters, Windsor, and the RenCen itself. Fishing piers and benches are scattered along the path. Rivard Plaza has a carousel, concessions, and bike rentals. Richard Plaza has covered seating, concessions, and a butterfly garden. As part of the longer riverfront route, the RiverWalk will ultimately span the distance from the Ambassador Bridge to Belle Isle. It is also helping to foster new retail and residential development.

A "lowland park" that is part of the larger Milliken Park is a demonstration of innovative landscaping that provides beauty and subtler environmental benefits. A constructed wetland filters 4.5 million gallons of surface runoff annually from 12.5 acres of properties adjacent to the park. It removes an anticipated 99 percent of sediment, 91 percent of phosphorus, 74 percent of nitrogen, 97 percent of lead, 91 percent of copper, and 87 percent of zinc from surface runoff from surrounding parcels. At the same time, it creates native habitat for sixty-two confirmed species of migratory and resident birds, including species dependent on wetlands. Over 450 trees and shrubs on the site sequester three tons of carbon annually.[9]

In the middle of the river, Belle Isle, formerly known as "Ile aux cochons" (hog or pig island), became one of the signature projects for Frederick Law Olmsted, the designer of Central Park in New York City. Motivated by "a strong belief in democracy," Olmsted sought to foster community, bringing Americans of diverse cultures together in "healthful outdoor settings." His specific Detroit design made "creative use of water and native plants along the water's edge." It was a visionary water-oriented park. Detroit—a city of great diversity positioned on water—was the perfect candidate to bring the public together on common ground in a beautiful setting in the river.[10]

The second oldest continuously operating rowing club property in the country occupies the island. Originally organized on the mainland, the Detroit Boat Club held races involving Belle Isle as early as 1840. In 1891 it began operations on the island; on August 4, 1902, the current boathouse was dedicated. It has fallen on hard times, though a dedicated band of rowers continue the tradition of racing sculls over the surface of the strait on the north side.

A major Belle Isle asset is the Dossin Great Lakes Museum. Located on "the Strand" along the Detroit River, the museum concentrates on Detroit's role in national and regional maritime history. It dates to 1961, when it replaced the City Maritime Museum aboard the *J.T. Wing* wooden schooner, the last commercial Great Lakes sailing ship. One of its most meaningful exhibits is the bow anchor of the *SS Edmund Fitzgerald*.

Belle Isle's renamed identity evokes the French heritage embedded so deeply along the lake plain. Other water-surrounded plots do the same: Peche Island upriver, Grosse Ile downriver, and Bois Blanc Island—more commonly known as simply "Boblo"—below Grosse Ile.

Birding is now thriving on the Detroit riverfront. Just east of the MacArthur Bridge to Belle Isle in Gabriel Richard Park are four wildlife spotting scopes and an interpretive panel identifying common birds that can be seen from the site. Educational programming promotes urban birding opportunities.

From Blight to Sight

Well into the twenty-first century, three cement silo complexes some seventeen stories tall constituted visual blight and prevented public access to the area between Woodward Avenue and Joseph Campau along the Detroit River. Symbols of the industrial use historically made of the East Riverfront, their existence literally blocked Detroit's future. Demolition would clear the way to unfold a new vision along the waterway, one prioritizing public access and residential development. More than three hundred acres of waterfront opportunity beckoned.[11] A "once-beautiful landscape" could reemerge.[12]

Integral to the re-visioning effort was a recent graduate of the University of Michigan Taubman College of Architecture and Urban Planning. Just twenty-five, former suburbanite Michael Cameron Dempsey dove into the complexity of the effort as a project manager at the Detroit Economic Growth Corporation. The newly hired planner was part of a core of young professionals at the DEGC dedicated to aiding Detroit's turnaround. "The goal," he told a news outlet, "is to create a traditional, walkable, good-looking, dense urban neighborhood" in place of blight.[13]

In August 2006 Dempsey made a presentation to and secured agreement by the Michigan Economic Growth Authority on the "transformational" nature of the project, thus enabling critical public/private financing to proceed. The resulting effort reshaped the land abutting the water into a vibrant urban area in which "abandoned and contaminated industrial sites along the immediate riverfront area will be reclaimed for productive use."[14] The rebirth of Detroit's riverfront required "pulling industrial sludge out of the ground."[15] By May 2007 the silos had been demolished, removing a critical impediment to "possibly one of the greatest areas of potential growth for the city."[16] The internationally acclaimed RiverWalk and other features of Detroit's rebirth soon began to take shape where large shadows had been cast over the land along the strait.

⌣

City investment in Detroit's riverfront resumed in earnest in 2016 in connection with Riverside Park on the southwest side of Detroit near the Ambassador Bridge. Baseball and soccer fields, basketball and volleyball courts, a picnic area, a skate park, and an amphitheater were all part of the plan to restore and reopen the park in early 2017 as a jewel along what has been a dilapidated area. One of the residents surveyed to provide input on improvements remarked, "I love water, so I love the idea that it's there."

Boblo and Belle Isle form two ends of the same waterborne spectrum. The latter had recreational aspects, notably placid lagoons and canals enabling persons of all physical abilities to get out on the water with little danger. The former had a more vigorous recreational approach, with rides and other amusements designed to excite and entertain. Opened in 1898, the Boblo park occupied an island that lies in Canadian waters near the mouth of the Detroit River. It was accessible for Americans only via excursion vessels, chiefly two steam-powered passenger ships commissioned as the *SS Columbia* and *SS Ste. Claire*. Both are National Register Historic Landmarks. The latter remains docked on the Rouge River undergoing restoration. Some twenty-five hundred passengers at a time took excursions on the Detroit River for a century before the park closed and the ships were mothballed.

As in Macomb County, some waterways here have also been put on mothballs and stored away.[17] There used to be an East Branch of the Rouge River, formed by the combination of three creeks: Campbell's, Holden, and Knagg's. By the turn of the twentieth century they had been "filled in and the 'made land' converted into city lots."[18] The Savoyard Creek is another lost river. Its origin was near the intersection of Riopelle Street and Congress (they no longer meet) on the east side of downtown, and it flowed under Woodward, where a favorite fishing hole existed and emptied into the main channel at the foot of Fourth Street, where the Riverfront Apartment complex now stands. Use as a sewer by residents condemned it to conversion into just that: the city "walled and covered it with stone."[19]

These postglacial and preimprovement streams are known today only because of histories written by those who did not want the early conditions of southeast Michigan to be lost to memory. They owe their fleeting remembrance to accounts and maps. One of the oldest was drawn by Douglass Houghton.[20]

From these efforts we can reminisce that south of the Rouge River was "in early days a chain or network of wet prairies ... once a fruitful field for the trapper. Beavers were plentiful here until about the beginning of the Nineteenth Century, when they disappeared. The early settlers cut large quantities of wild hay from these wet lands to provide sustenance for their live stock during the long, cold winters."[21]

While those qualities might never return, a modern-day amenity is already in place. As Detroit emerged from bankruptcy in late 2014, the state Department of Natural Resources played a significant role in promoting public access to and enjoyment of river-related attractions. "Rich with history and natural beauty," says DNR publicity, Belle Isle Park became Michigan's 102d state park that year as part of a lease agreement with the City of Detroit. Enlisting the aid of private groups, the DNR has made significant investments to bring the park back to its glory. The Michigan historical marker's opening line thus may be revived: "This island, a jewel in the hearts of Detroiters, has provided shining memories for visitors of all ages."

The Detroit/Wayne County Port Authority and the Dossin Great Lakes Museum have divergent missions, yet one thing in common: each displays a twelve-hundred-pound artifact recovered from the bed of the Detroit River: British cannons dating from the eighteenth century. The most recent cannon discovery was made in 2011 by a police diver during training at the bottom of the river. Embossed with the crest of King George II, the weapon was fabricated in East Sussex, England, in the mid-1740s, according to the Detroit Historical Society. Along with its companions, it was disposed of in the river when the British evacuated Fort Lernoult in 1796. Preserved for two centuries in the riverbed, the artillery piece adds to the lore of the city's early history.

The conflict of priorities has always been an issue along the Detroit River. Business and commercial interests enjoy support for the jobs they bring to a sometimes-struggling regional economy. But there is support, too, for the utilitarian and aesthetic values associated with natural resources conservation. The question is whether decision-makers will be smart and skillful enough to promote and balance both values.

Pollution and industrial activity have long been persistent concerns in southwest Detroit. The neighborhood was once a well-populated community where workers could walk to their job locations at the mills and warehouses and foundries and shops that gave economic vibrancy to the area. Detroit helped build the middle class; its manufacturing was once the envy of the world for the quality of living it produced, if not the environmental impact.

What did Detroit make before it made cars? *Lots* of things: stoves, lumber, salt, ships, spirits, tobacco, pharmaceuticals, and more, each product pushing Detroit's pin on the map a little deeper, enticing a few more people to pack up their worldly belongings and head to the city to try something new.[22]

Along the East Riverfront still exist the remnants of one of the world's most prolific drug manufacturers. Parke-Davis and Company was founded in Detroit by Dr. Samuel P. Duffield, a physician and pharmacist. In 1860, Dr. Duffield owned a drugstore at the corner of Gratiot and Woodward Avenues, where he made a variety of pharmaceutical preparations. A partnership of Dr. Duffield and Hervey Coke Parke was formed in October 1866, and the company was launched. The next year, a partner was added to aid in sales—George S. Davis. In 1871 the Parke-Davis brand was born when Duffield retired. Over the next century, the company became one of the world's largest concerns.

The company's first manufacturing plant was located in downtown Detroit, but in the 1870s new manufacturing facilities at Joseph Campau Street and the river took the original's place. Access to water and rail transportation was a key advantage of the site. Between 1891 and 1955, the company expanded the complex to cover over fourteen acres in twenty-six structures. Some of Detroit's most prominent architects, including Donaldson and Meier, Albert Kahn, and Smith, Hinchman and Grylls, contributed their designs. Perhaps the most notable building is the first industrial research laboratory in the nation established for the specific purpose of conducting pharmacological research. The structure was declared a National Historic Landmark in 1976. After Parke Davis departed the complex, the Stroh Real Estate firm took charge of the site and converted many of the buildings into amenities, including offices, condos, and a hotel. Now known as Stroh River Place, the complex thrives with its mix of office, residential, and commercial uses.

In the 1850s, the S.D. Elwood & Company offices stood at the corner of Jefferson Avenue and Bates Street in Detroit (the intersection today is where the Coleman A. Young Municipal Center, Jefferson, and Hart Plaza meet). As publishers, importers. and dealers in foreign and American books and stationery, the company ambit was far-reaching. In 1852, nineteen-year-old Dexter Mason Ferry secured employment there as errand boy and was, by 1856, listed as an accountant in the city. That same year, he heard the entrepreneurial calling and helped found the firm of "M.T. Gardner & Company, seedsmen." In 1865 the enterprise became known as Ferry, Church & Company and in 1867 simply as "D.M. Ferry & Company."

The changes reflected Ferry's continuing exercise of successful skill in growing the seed business and helping make Detroit the seed capital of the world. "Distinctively a man with ideas and ideals," Ferry "did not narrow his mental horizon within the bounds of personal advancement and aggrandizement."[23] By 1890 the Ferry seed enterprise did more than $1.5 million in sales, supplying seed packets to retail stores and through its mail order catalog. From the center of Detroit and relying on its farms throughout the city and elsewhere, this southeast Michigan seed enterprise brought on innovations such as brightly colored seed packets and relied on a reputation for quality seed with tested high germination rates to help spur sales.

Urban farming drew much attention during the run-up to Detroit's 2013 bankruptcy. In its aftermath, the number of firms, projects, and acreage devoted to growing and harvesting urban food multiplied. The Greening of Detroit nonprofit organization sought to turn vacant land into places for growing food and putting Detroiters to work. Originally organized to respond to the demise of American elm trees in the city, the agency sought to increase the planting of trees and creation of green open spaces, prairies, urban farms, and pocket parks. Another major player was Hantz Farms, which proclaimed: "We can build a new, green economy in Detroit, and lead the world by example."

Henry Ford once sought to lead by example and sustain a green, decentralized economic model with his cottage industry factories that populated southeast Michigan's rivers. Also known as Ford's village industries, these rural plants manufactured small automotive parts at dispersed locations on the streams and rivers of the region. Around 1918, Ford began purchasing grist mills along the Rouge River and converted them into manufacturing facilities powered by hydroelectricity. Many employees were farmers who worked in the factories after the farming season concluded.

A number of these structures still exist and are in use. The Nankin Mills, thirty miles upstream from the mouth of the Rouge, was the first Ford purchased. In 1920, the mill began making screws and was later retooled for the production of stencils. During World War II, Nankin Mills turned out parts for the B-24 bomber being manufactured at Willow Run Airport. Located on Edward Hines Drive near Ann Arbor Trail and Joy Road, it is today a Wayne County Interpretive Center. Further west, the Newburg Mill, the Wilcox Mill, the Phoenix Mill, and others still stand.

The Detroit riverfront was once primarily industry territory. Railroads terminated there. Silos and warehouses dominated. Numerous ships tied up there. Today, industry's presence is most clearly manifested by the long ships that continue to ply the strait. Today's merchant fleet towers over the diminutive *Griffon*, the first European-constructed ship to maneuver through the waterway connecting Lakes Erie and Huron. The Lake Carriers' Association represents fifteen US-flag vessel operators on the Great Lakes, with fifty-six self-propelled vessels and tug/barge units. These ships range in length from just under five hundred feet, almost as tall as the Penobscot Building in downtown Detroit, to over one thousand feet—taller than the seventy-three-story hotel structure in the middle of the RenCen. Total annual tonnage shipped via these vessels exceeded 100 million tons in 2015, consisting of cement, coal, grain, iron ore, limestone, salt, and sand.

Added to this domestic fleet are the oceangoing "salties" under Swiss, Dutch, German, Greek, and other foreign ownership. These ships arrive from faraway ports and add to the romance of the seas. Since 1959, when the Saint Lawrence Seaway system opened to their commerce, they have transported cargo worth more than $300 billion.[24] The salties have also contributed to a major problem for the waterways of the Great Lakes, the introduction of invasive species that threaten native fisheries and habitats. The Great Lakes ecosystem has been severely damaged by more than 180 invasive and nonnative varieties: the zebra mussel, quagga mussel, and round goby are among species that colonized the lakes after being dumped out with ballast water taken on in faraway ports. Many of these creatures "reproduce and spread, ultimately degrading habitat, out-competing native species, and short-circuiting food webs." The good news is that after the widespread implementation of ballast water exchange in 2006, far fewer aquatic invasive species were introduced to the Great Lakes through ballast.

The river provides a convenient passageway between nations and is at the heart of the largest international trade corridor in North America. Two bridges, three rail tunnels, and two truck ferries crossing the Detroit and St. Clair Rivers carry more than 25 percent of the approximately $750 billion per year trade between the United States and Canada, by far America's largest trading partner. This includes more than 4 million trucks per year and the number two and three rail ports in the United States, carrying goods on a transportation network that flows throughout the United States and Canada. More than 15 million passenger vehicles also cross between southeast Michigan and southwest Ontario every year. Another 60 million tons of shipping per year transits under these bridges.

So central is the international crossing to southwest Ontario to trade, commuting, and tourism between Canada and the United States that a bridge financed entirely by Canada is scheduled to begin service by 2020. Named the Gordie Howe International Bridge for Detroit's longtime National Hockey League star, this crossing will provide another landmark for Detroit's water renaissance.

There is more good news; the water quality of the Detroit River and its tributaries—the source of disease that killed thousands in the early twentieth century—has recovered dramatically. It is now clean enough to support the rebound of the prehistoric lake sturgeon and creation of the world's first international wildlife refuge. Both notions come together down the river.

Fort Wayne

At the narrowest point of the Detroit River sits a crumbling fortress erected in the 1840s as a key to America's homeland security. Its masonry walls are dilapidated; many of its buildings have fallen into disrepair or been demolished. Historic Fort Wayne has stood guard along southeast Michigan's freshwater coast and flown the American flag faithfully for nearly nineteen decades. Its heritage dates back to the Native peoples.

Unlike much of the riverfront along Michigan's largest city, the spot at which the western portion of the fort property meets the water is free of concrete. Standing along the shore, one can imagine how the earliest human arrivals via canoe made their landing here, constructed a settlement, lived their lives in tune with nature, and venerated their dead in a burial mound that has survived a millennium down to the present. These thousand feet of grassy shore illustrate the original nature of the strait.

In the early nineteenth century, the US government gained control over the Michigan Territory, Michigan become a state, and tensions with Canada persisted. Securing the border became a priority. An act of Congress approved by President John Tyler on September 9, 1841, provided $50,000 for "defensive works, and barracks, and purchase of site at or near Detroit, Michigan." In 1842, the army dispatched Lieutenant Montgomery C. Meigs, later of Civil War fame, to Detroit, where he acquired several ribbon farms in the Springwells area and acted as supervising engineer for construction of an earthen fort. Congress made further appropriations over succeeding years until completion of the structure in 1852.

Meigs chose the site for strategic military value. On elevated ground that commanded the Detroit River and the opposite Canadian shoreline, the fort's location ensured that hostile forces could not pass upriver or prevent US vessels from traveling along this part of the border.

No war with Canada came. Instead, the fort served during the Civil War as mustering site for some fourteen thousand Michigan soldiers. It was upgraded to a stone-walled star fort, one of the "Third System" period fortifications that comprised a more sophisticated approach to defense. It would play an active role as an induction center for thousands of recruits in subsequent wars, concluding with the Vietnam War.

During the Great Depression, its housing stock provided a haven for Detroit's homeless. The Works Progress Administration gave employment to many who helped restore and improve the facility. The fort was a mobilization center for those in the Civilian Conservation Corps. Such social welfare efforts served as precedent for the fort's use in the latter part of the twentieth century by the Mosaic Youth Theater, Detroit Head Start, and the National Museum of the Tuskegee Airmen.

In the 1940s it was a vital part of the Arsenal of Democracy. Armaments and vehicles produced in the Detroit-area manufacturing plants were brought here for shipment to the front. The site served as launch control and supply point for the ring of Nike missiles that protected Michigan from Soviet attack during the 1950s and early 1960s. Finally, in the 1970s it gave up its military character and became largely a museum piece.

For all of these reasons, the site is on the National Register of Historic Places and the Michigan State Historical Sites Registry.

In late January 2015, HR&A Advisors of New York City was hired for $235,000 by the Michigan Economic Development Corporation to devise a plan to retain the site's historic attributes while exploring other uses, such as housing, offices, and industrial or cultural development. Impetus for the study arose from the Gordie Howe International Bridge project. A $250–$300 million US customs plaza for the new bridge will be constructed across Jefferson Avenue from Fort Wayne.

A federal government installation, the Detroit Area Office of the US Army Corps of Engineers, bars the way between the fort's southeast-facing bastion and the waterway.

On one of the very few remaining natural portals to the river, Fort Wayne's historic infrastructure bears the impact of decades of government neglect. "No hostile shots have ever been fired" here, reads the 1977 Michigan historical marker, as worn as the bastion it commemorates.

Within the compound of Fort Wayne is one of the few remaining undisturbed Indian mounds in a region where there were many. As with communities that came to Michigan from other parts of the world, the Native peoples paid honor to their deceased family members near the homes of the living.

A Native American village was observable on the site in the 1700s. The National Register and a National Landmark proposal date settlement at the site back to AD 650. A 1768 map at the Detroit Public Library's Burton Collection shows the site as occupied by a Potawatomi Indian village. This tribe was one of four invited by Cadillac in 1710 to settle near the fort at Detroit for the French fur trade.

The "Western Gazetteer or Emigrants Directory" published in 1817 described the Springwells burial mounds. During 1842–1845, the US Army and its contractors destroyed a central burial mound on the grounds during construction of the fort. In 1876, with US government permission, a Harvard University archaeologist began excavating the remaining burial mound and wrote an extensive report on his findings. In 1944–1945 the army permitted complete excavation of the remaining mound.[*]

Government desecration of indigenous heritage sites has prompted policy change in recent years, including the 1990 Native American Graves Protection and Repatriation Act, and proposed Michigan legislation.

In 2016, signs of hope emerged. The National Park Service began working with the City of Detroit to develop a comprehensive strategic plan for the fort. A $265,000 grant from the Kresge Foundation funded a consultant to identify the current state of the grounds and buildings, and develop suggestions to increase public access to the grounds.

---

*From the National Historic Landmark draft submission compiled by James Conway, Fort Wayne project manager and historian, July 2010.

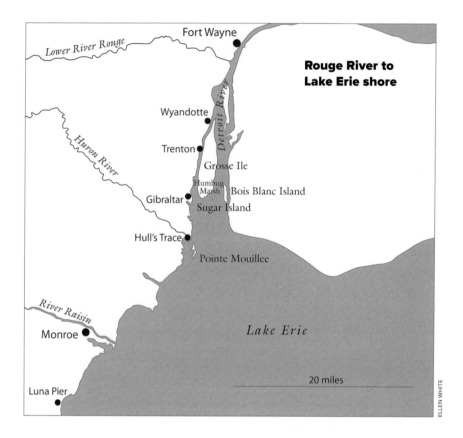

Fort Wayne

Lower River Rouge

**Rouge River to
Lake Erie shore**

Detroit River

Wyandotte

Huron River

Trenton

Grosse Ile

Humbug
Marsh   Bois Blanc Island

Gibraltar

Sugar Island

Hull's Trace

Pointe Mouillee

River Raisin

Monroe

Lake Erie

20 miles

Luna Pier

ELLEN WHITE

CHAPTER 5

Downriver

Paddle stayed a week in Detroit. Ore boats unloaded their red ore beside the factory that would turn it into thousands of bright new automobiles. At the end of his week Paddle again went in the motorboat with the girl and her father, this time down the Detroit River. Ferryboats running between the United States and Canada chugged across their bow. Canoes with picnickers, rowboats with silent fishermen, passenger steamers noisy with dance music, passed by. Big buildings dropped astern. Green fields replaced them, and a Coast Guard station, trim and white, and islands with lighthouses. Then the shore dropped away and the motorboat stopped. There was a splash.

"Here's Lake Erie, Paddle-to-the-Sea," cried the girl. "Good-by and good luck."

—Holling C. Holling, *Paddle to the Sea*, 1941

The waters and adjacent lands south of what is now Detroit are a two-way street of time and place. They have been both a battleground and a hunting and fishing ground. Because they are downstream of the heart of the lakes, they are sometimes forgotten—but they are a critical part of the region. And they have an identity all their own.

Detroit's "downriver" connotes blue collars, muskrats, and smokestacks. Because many industrial facilities were located there, close to the water and its transportation, many factory and warehouse workers made their homes here. It is not, however, a cultural backwater any more than it is a natural backwater. The Downriver Council for the Arts, a regional arts organization and public gallery proudly flying the downriver flag, serves twenty-one communities, over 350,000 people, and sixty-five cultural groups. Dan Featherstone, a published poet who grew up in the area, credits his youth there with a major influence: "My sustained interest in the natural world is influenced by those pockets of nature that persist there—wetlands, woods and, of course, the Detroit River."[1]

Seven downriver municipalities border the Detroit River: Brownstown Township, Ecorse, Gibraltar, River Rouge, Riverview, Trenton, and Wyandotte. Add in an eighth for good measure: Grosse Ile, the island community in the middle of the Detroit River.

Grosse Ile

Seven miles long and a mile and one-half wide, Grosse Ile is the largest of the Detroit River islands and has a population of approximately 104,000. It is actually not a single, solid land mass. A number of smaller islands surround the main. The Thorofare Canal bisects the main island, running from the main channel of the Detroit River on the east into the Trenton Channel next to the mainland on the west. Hennepin Point, named to honor seventeenth-century French explorer Father Louis Hennepin, is located on the tip of the main island's northern section and is the site of the Grosse Ile lighthouse.

William Macomb built his "Mansion House" on the river side in 1783–1784. Nearby, he operated a horse-driven grist mill from 1787 until about

1840. According to the nearby historical marker, "Ten acres were cleared and enclosed as meadows for the mill horses. Equipped with 'a pair of Stones 3 feet 3 inches in diameter,'" the mill and a "Cyder Press" were maintained near the shore along with a wharf from which to ship his product. The US military maintained a stockade on the Canadian side toward the lower point of the island from 1815 to 1817. The fort was abandoned in 1819. In addition to the Macomb family, several French families settled Grosse Ile in those early years, including the Reaumes and Charles Boucher, whose descendants still occupied parts of the old farms in the early 1900s.

Elisabeth Denison, also known as Lisette, was born a slave in Macomb County in 1786. She gained her freedom by moving to Canada and returned a free person thanks to a judicial ruling. She worked in Detroit for several prominent families, and in 1856 began working for William S. Biddle at his estate on Grosse Ile. With careful financial management, she was able to invest in land. At her death, her will provided funds to build Saint James Episcopal Chapel. With supplemental funds from William and his brother James, a Gothic chapel was constructed in the summer of 1867 that remains standing.

As Detroit River traffic grew, the Cleveland Vessel Owners Association petitioned Congress for authorization and funding for the erection of navigation lights that would enable ships to operate around the clock. In 1891, range lights were installed on Hennepin Point to guide up-bound ships past the sandbar off Fighting Island. In 1894, the government installed another set, the Grosse Ile North Channel Range Lights, to serve down-bound traffic. This light resembled a water tower on stilts because of its construction on wooden pilings. The structure was rebuilt in 1906 and is the only remaining lighthouse on the island.

Evidence of what was once a major water feature of Grosse Ile—the Wonder Well—has vanished. In 1903, Sinclair Company drillers seeking oil found mineral water instead. Located on the southern part of Grosse Ile off Southpointe Drive, the 2,375-foot-deep well was a veritable gusher, producing a natural artesian flow of two million gallons of water a day at its peak. It was said to pump fifty-two-degree water as high as twenty-two feet in the air. As with other mineral-rich waters, the Wonder Well's bounty was bottled and sold for its purportedly medicinal qualities, especially for stomach woes. Profiled in Ripley's *Believe It or Not* and appearing in the AAA tourist guide, the well's flow began to diminish in the 1950s. The Wonder Well ran dry in 1994. The adjoining property was vacated in the early 2000s, and demolition was completed in 2014.[2]

A local nonprofit organization, the Grosse Ile Nature and Land Conservancy, has protected 41 acres on the main island and there are 566 acres of protected open space and 121 acres of marshland and conservation easements, also on the main island. The Michigan Department of Natural Resources owns 365 acres on the adjacent islands. Although the land is not open to the public, migratory birds and other wildlife can make use of another 225 acres at the northern tip of the island, including Hennepin Point. Once used by BASF Corporation's predecessor companies as a dumping ground for by-products from chemical manufacturing, the site has been secured and is being rehabilitated and revegetated by the company.

Sugar Island

Named for the sugar maple trees growing on its shores, Sugar Island is located between Grosse Ile and Bois Blanc/Boblo islands. Sugar Island once featured an amusement park with a roller coaster, dance pavilion, baseball diamond, and swimming beach. Steamers including the side wheeler *Tashmoo* once carried excursioners here from communities along the Detroit River.

The White Star line launched the *Tashmoo*, built at the Wyandotte shipyards, to ferry passengers between Detroit and Port Huron. Later, the vessel made trips on a downriver swing that included Sugar Island and Lake Erie. On the evening cruise of June 18, 1936, while carrying fourteen hundred passengers, the *Tashmoo* struck a submerged rock at the mouth of the Sugar Island Channel. The captain maneuvered the stricken vessel to the closest safe haven, a coal dock on the Amherstburg, Ontario side. There were no casualties. The only impact was on the patronage of Sugar Island. Nearby Bob-Lo Island Park soon took over as the preferred destination, and the buildings and rides fell into disrepair. In 1954, the dance pavilion burned to the ground to end the era.

In 2012 the Fish and Wildlife Service acquired Sugar Island as an addition to the Detroit River International Wildlife Refuge. The west beach is open dawn to dusk from Memorial Day to Labor Day.

Wyandotte

The area that became the city of Wyandotte was first settled in 1732 by a branch of the Huron tribe known as the Wyandots. Also known as the Wendat, this tribe centered at the north end shore of Lake Ontario before migrating to Georgian Bay, where they encountered the French explorer Samuel de Champlain in 1615.

The Wyandots arrived when their French allies founded Detroit, inhabiting a village variously rendered as Maquaqua or Monguagon. Major John Biddle, a US Army officer during the War of 1812, established a farm called "The Wyandotte" in honor of his neighbors, and from this the community derived its name. The village founding coincided with establishment of its first major business, the Eureka Iron Works. It was the first mill in the nation to produce steel based on the Bessemer process. Ore shipped from upper Michigan was smelted into steel in furnaces that were heated by charcoal made from wood cut in the surrounding forests. The Wyandotte Shipyards commenced operation in 1871. The shipyard produced the *Tashmoo* and the *Columbia*, one of the Boblo boats.

The Lower Detroit River segment of the Detroit River Heritage Water Trail begins in Wyandotte's Bishop Park, the ten-mile segment running to Lake Erie. It is one of four trail segments beginning at Belle Isle and including portions of the Rouge and Huron Rivers. In turn, the Detroit River Trail is part of a larger Michigan Great Lakes Water Trails system, whose goal is to link regional water trails to form a statewide water trail system along every mile of Great Lakes shoreline.

Trenton

The original name of the township, across the channel from the center of Grosse Ile, was Monguagon, dubbed by territorial governor Lewis Cass for the Wyandot village. In 1828 its post office bore the name Monguago. The name was changed to Truago in 1837. Finally, in 1847, the present name was adopted in recognition of the limestone strata underlying the town.

The community was the site of the War of 1812 Battle of Monguagon. On August 9, 1812, a force of six hundred American troops moved up the Hull's Trace, a makeshift road, in an attempt to bring desperately needed supplies from Frenchtown (today's Monroe) to Detroit. Near the Wyandot village, the American scouts collided with a British and Indian force. In the heavy fighting, the British were driven across the Detroit River, while Native forces withdrew into nearby woods. The victory did not prevent the US surrender of Detroit a week later.

Originally erected in 1962, the Michigan historical marker that told this tale was replaced in August 2012, following a fund-raising effort led by the Daughters of the American Revolution. The text was revised to provide a more accurate historical understanding of the Native American involvement.

Operated by DTE Energy, the Trenton Channel Power Plant, fired by coal, has been one of the most prominent structures in the area, its twin striped stacks towering over the Detroit River. In 2016 two of three remaining generating units closed, leaving only one of the original nine. The utility shut down the units in part because of their age and inefficiency and in part to comply with new federal rules cracking down on mercury and greenhouse gas emissions from coal plants. The company said the 2016 closings would cost no jobs.

Accessed from a launch at Wayne County's Elizabeth Park or by standing on the shore, Trenton Channel is a popular spot for fishing. Typical sport fish species in the channel include catfish, largemouth bass, northern pike, smallmouth bass, sunfish, walleye, white bass, and yellow perch.

One major step toward renewing Trenton's water resources is embodied in a name change—from the Black Lagoon to Ellias Cove. For decades, industries dumped oil, grease, and chemicals that ultimately reached an inlet that then turned black. With federal Great Lakes Legacy Act funds, cleanup crews removed 115,000 cubic yards of polluted sludge from the lagoon. This captured more than 470,000 pounds of contaminants, including 160 pounds of PCBs, 38,000 pounds of lead, 360 pounds of mercury, 300,000 pounds of oil and grease, and 140,000 pounds of zinc. Subsequent work restored wildlife habitat around the Black Lagoon. In 2007, the city of Trenton officially renamed the lagoon Ellias Cove, after the family that donated adjacent land in honor of the successful restoration effort.[3]

Gibraltar

Like its sister community to the north, this town was the site of a War of 1812 clash. On August 5, six weeks after the outbreak of war, a Native force led by the famous Shawnee chief Tecumseh attacked an American party heading south. Their objective was Frenchtown, where supplies vital to the American troops in Detroit awaited. The plan was to secure and transport the supplies back north through Indian country. Tecumseh's men opened fire as the unsuspecting Americans forded Brownstown Creek. The Americans were routed. Seventeen Americans were killed, twelve wounded, and two captured. One Native American was killed.

Gibraltar's name reflects its platting in 1837 by trustees of the Gibraltar & Flat Rock Company. The company's vision was to sell pricy lots and reap the profits. The scheme failed. The land went back to a more sustainable, more realistic use: farming.[4]

Gibraltar's municipal website touts the city's "significant number of natural resources, including a network of more than five miles of canals, wetlands and streams." The canals bisect the city and its four islands: Hall, Edmund, Main, and Horse. West of the canals and north of Lake Erie Metropark is a fifteen-acre property known as Six Points that descendants of the initial inhabitants reclaimed in 2015. The Wyandotte Nation of Oklahoma purchased the land for members of the tribe in southeast Michigan and southwestern Ontario, the Wyandot of Anderdon Nation. It is the only communal land in what was once home for an entire nation.[5] Containing about 8.5 acres of wetlands, the land lies close to the confluence of Marsh Creek and the Detroit River. The Wyandot plan to build a traditional longhouse, acquire artifacts and repatriate ancestors' bones from the University of Michigan and Wayne State University for reinternment, and create walking trails for nonindigenous people as well as a culturally significant "medicine walk" trail to be used by the Wyandot for healing purposes.

Humbug Marsh

Jefferson Avenue north of Gibraltar is a study in contrasts. On the west side sit hulks of factories and warehouses that produced heavy goods and harsh pollution but afforded workers a standard of living that helped establish Michigan's middle class. Their silence today is testimony to the changes wrought, beginning in the 1970s, by a global economy. No longer could a Michigander drop out of high school, work in one of the many industrial establishments of the region, and end up with a comfortable residence in southeast Michigan, a cottage up north or on one of the nearby lakes or rivers, and a truck to carry the worker and family between them. Downriver had to adjust.

On the east side of Jefferson, though, is a dramatically different scene. No steel sheds loom; no smokestacks rise toward the sky. One must get to 5437 West Jefferson Avenue, looking north to the stacks of the DTE coal plant and the Solutia plastic fabrication facility, to see industry's presence. Here is the entrance to the only truly undisturbed portion of the Detroit River, a trip back in time to when the indigenous population called it home.

Making a turn into the entrance took one to a construction site in 2016. The builders were constructing not a factory, but a nature reserve. At over four hundred acres, the Humbug Marsh unit of the Detroit River International Wildlife Refuge is a testament to good fortune. Somehow, through nearly three centuries of Western occupation, this frontage on the river has remained undisturbed. It is the last mile of natural shoreline along the US mainland portion of the Detroit River.

In the mid-1990s, a developer acquired the site to build a subdivision, marina, golf course, bridge to Humbug Island to accommodate homes, and more. But area residents, conservationists, government agencies, and nonprofit organizations joined together to prevent the loss of this irreplaceable natural habitat, a millennia-old link to the region's freshwater heritage that can be cherished now and forever. Wayne County acquired the site in 2002.

A Gold Leadership in Energy and Environmental Design (LEED)-certified visitor center, opened in 2019, welcomes guests. It demonstrates the power of cleanup and restoration of an industrial brownfield into the Refuge Gateway. Formerly operated as a Chrysler manufacturing facility, the site will serve as hub for environmental education, outdoor recreational activities, and sustainability. "Everything visitors see and do at the Refuge Gateway and visitor center will teach them how to live sustainably," says the official documentation.

In 2010, Humbug Marsh received a designation as a "Wetland of International Importance" from the international Ramsar Convention.[6] Only thirty-seven such sites exist in the United States; Humbug Marsh was the first in Michigan. The site merited designation because of its ecological importance in the Detroit River corridor and the Great Lakes Basin ecosystem.

Despite state antipollution laws passed in 1948, by the 1960s phosphorus fouled the Detroit River and nearby Lake Erie. Faced with declining fish

Humbug Marsh

Conservation lands are usually more than pretty places. In an area as intensely developed as downriver Detroit, that is especially true. It turns out that a rare piece of natural land fiercely fought over in the 1990s, and now part of the Detroit River International Wildlife Refuge, has values that weren't known at the time it was protected.

Humbug Marsh, almost obliterated for development in the late 1990s, was a principal investigation site for botanists Brad Slaughter and Mike Penskar of the Michigan Natural Features Inventory in 2015. The two scientists searched for the unique and critical in small forest stands that total less than five hundred acres on the Humbug site. They also investigated forests at Oakwoods Metropark and on Grosse Ile.

The baseline for the scientists' work was a set of old land records from the federal government's General Land Office. Joseph Fletcher walked what is today Humbug Marsh in 1817, noting details about the native forest, mainly for the purpose of documenting timber values. Slaughter and Penskar looked carefully for features of the forest that persisted after two hundred years of intensive land use.

The impact of such use has been felt all along the Huron-to-Erie corridor. In 1879, Bela Hubbard spoke of the corridor's state as seen by the Europeans two centuries previous: "The natural beauty of the region lying between Lakes Erie and Huron has been recorded by all the early travelers, with words of admiration. Many of the islands were low, and some of the river margins scarcely above the water. But all was green and peaceful. Dark forests extended to the river edge, and many and many a tall monarch of the wood waved its gigantic arms over the brink, and was reflected in the glassy surface which not tide or flood ever disturbed. The marshes were luxuriant with wild rice that furnished a sumptuous repast to a great variety of birds and waterfowl, and even a welcoming supply to the Indians. Occasional villages and bark wigwams enlivened the shore, surrounded with gardens and cornfields, and the most elevated points were crowned with burial grounds. Most of the shores had high banks and were covered with timber."*

John Gannon, retired senior scientist at the International Joint Commission's Windsor office, says researchers have found maps from the early 1800s showing large stretches of the Detroit River had extensive wetlands a mile wide. "Can you imagine the amount of biodiversity lost as European pioneers developed farms and channelized the river for shipping, docks, and other uses? The earliest accounts of European explorers indicated that the area was a haven for fish and wildlife," he said.†

Among the most notable features of the corridor's coastal zone were expanses of marshes distinct to the Great Lakes, and much diminished today. Wild rice, now listed as threatened in Michigan, was common. Species of birds now rare in the region, the king rail, black tern, and least bittern, thrived in the habitat. The Detroit River has lost 97 percent of its coastal marshes, and comparable losses have occurred on the shorelines of Lake St. Clair and the St. Clair River. But governments and private parties are gaining momentum in efforts to restore and connect marshes with the larger ecosystem.

So natural reservoirs of biological diversity grow in importance. Although the Humbug finds aren't household names, botanists were excited by the discoveries, including a rare grass-like plant called the hairy-fruited sedge (*Carex trichocarpa*) and an orchid species called oval ladies'-tresses (*Spiranthes ovalis*) never before found in Wayne County.

Grosse Ile also yielded two species of special concern, including a sedge known as *Carex Squarrosa*, which had not been found there since 1932, and the Shumard oak, never recorded on the island, which was determined to be the dominant tree on the island's remaining forest.

In fact, Grosse Ile is one of the strongholds in southeast Michigan for the Shumard oak, which the state has classified as a species of special concern, one step short of "threatened."

That's not to say the site has been untouched by human development. Penskar, coinvestigator of the assessment, observed that Humbug has been "hammered. A lot of tough love is needed to get the place under control, and there are many invasives including even native species such as very aggressive dogwood shrubs that need to be controlled to give the natural flora more of a competitive advantage and a chance to establish. The woods need a good deal of invasive work in spots."

Restoring Humbug Marsh to thriving biodiversity would be a long and costly project. Yet the fact that it is even possible to discuss is an unlikely development after two hundred years of intensive land alteration in the region.

Greg Norwood, the refuge biologist, said, "The species that make up places like Humbug Marsh are perhaps analogous to collections of books in a library—there are those shelves made up of mostly old, rare books that have somehow been left unchanged, collecting dust together for decades."

Although the sites did not contain a large number of threatened and endangered species, they do serve as "important reservoirs of plant diversity," the two scientists said. They also serve as reservoirs of quiet beauty, and quiet itself, in the tumultuous daily routine of southeast Michigan.

---

*Quoted in US Fish and Wildlife Service, "Along the Shoreline," https://www.fws.gov/uploadedFiles/Along_the_Shoreline.pdf.

†John Gannon, personal communication, May 2, 2017.

populations and unhealthy waters, Michigan set strict limits on phosphates in laundry detergent. The 1970 discovery of industrial mercury in the river encouraged passage of the US Clean Water Act and the US-Canada Great Lakes Water Quality Agreement, both signed in 1972. Pollution control and prevention measures resulted in increased reproduction among sturgeon and whitefish in the Detroit River and the return of peregrine falcons and bald eagles along its banks.

A Michigan historical marker standing in front of the visitor center entrance emphasizes the area's environmental recovery. Present at the marker dedication on Labor Day weekend 2007 were public servants proud of the success of the combined forces that had preserved the region's heritage here, among them refuge manager John Hartig, Congressman John D. Dingell, and Wayne County executive Robert Ficano.

The Detroit River International Wildlife Refuge

In 2000, a group of Canadian and US conservationists and scientists drafted a conservation vision for the downriver ecosystem that called for creation of an international wildlife refuge—the first in the world. Longtime area congressman John Dingell introduced legislation to establish the refuge, and President George W. Bush signed the authorizing legislation in December 2001.

The refuge zone extends forty-eight miles along the shoreline of the Detroit River and western Lake Erie. Its freshwater marshes near a major urban metroplex distinguish the area from all others in the Great Lakes Basin and in America. Nearly 7 million people live within a forty-five-minute drive of the refuge. Studies have demonstrated that outdoor recreation in the only international heritage river system in North America contributes millions of dollars to the local economy. On the Canadian side the Western Lake Erie Watersheds Priority Natural Area stretches from Peche Isle at the head of the Detroit River, through the mouth of the Detroit River to Ontario waters of western Lake Erie, including Point Pelee National Park and Pelee Island.

The refuge focuses on conserving, protecting, and restoring habitat for 300 species of birds and 117 species of fish. Within the refuge zone is a treasury of species, including 30 waterfowl species, 23 of raptors, and 31 of shorebirds. The refuge currently owns or cooperatively manages 5,834 acres of unique habitats. The international designation is supported by a Canadian registry of lands that includes 3,797 acres owned by the Essex Region Conservation Authority and 981 acres owned by the City of Windsor. Between Canada and United States, 18,877 acres of land in southwest Ontario and southeast Michigan are now being managed as part of the refuge. The goal is 25,000 acres in the next ten years.

John Hartig, manager of the refuge and author of a book on the recovery of the Detroit River and three other industrial rivers, observes that "during the 1960s, the Detroit River was considered one of the most polluted rivers in North America because of its long history of industrial and urban development that led to unsustainable human use and abuse of this ecosystem." "Today," he adds, "the environmental cleanup and revival of the river has led to one of the most remarkable ecological recovery stories in North America." Particularly notable is the return of bald eagles, peregrine falcons, osprey, lake sturgeon, lake whitefish, walleye, wild celery, mayflies, beaver, and other species.[7]

The recovery of whitefish in the River is remarkable. In 1824, a commercial fishing operation caught thirty thousand off Grosse Ile in one day. But relentless fishing of the species drove down populations during the latter half of the 1800s. When workers dredged the riverbed for navigation in 1913, they wiped out whitefish spawning grounds. It would be ninety-three years before whitefish were confirmed as spawning in the river again.[8]

Signals of progress include the steep decline in phosphorus concentrations and discharges from Detroit's sewage treatment plant, the elimination of four thousand tons per day of chloride dumping in the Detroit River, and the removal of nearly a million cubic meters of contaminated sediments, costing over $154 million.

The Erie Marsh Preserve is one of the protected areas of the refuge. In 1858, construction of the Detroit-Toledo Railroad impacted the natural marsh that had flourished since the glaciers had withdrawn. By 1898, two more rail lines had been laid on causeways through the marshes, cutting off much of the marsh from its Lake Erie connection. Agriculture took over, leaving only a few remnants. Construction of I-75 in 1958 under federal sponsorship erected a further dam across the alluvium. Only the stubborn efforts of duck hunters, for whom the marsh was not a swamp but a paradise, saved the marsh. The Erie Shooting and Fishing Club, founded in 1870, began in 1950 to restore the natural action of Erie's ebb and flow. The work is monumental, requiring construction of dikes, water pumps, natural plantings, prescribed burnings and sprayings, and persistence in the face of many obstacles.[9]

And yet in the midst of it all is a spring some 440 million years old. The "Great Sulphur Spring" is shown on early maps of Lake Erie and has resisted all of humanity's efforts at obliteration through the centuries. The source is a Silurian bedrock aquifer;[10] "the outlet from the spring is a small sized river having considerable velocity."[11]

Huron River

The Huron River enters Lake Erie just below the mouth of the Detroit River. Approximately 130 miles long, the Huron drains 908 square miles of land and drops more than 400 feet from its headwaters near Indian Springs Metropark, nine miles west of Pontiac, on its run to Lake Erie. At Lower Huron Metropark, in the crook of the arm formed by the I-94/I-275 cloverleaf, "is the last substantial piece of the bottomland hardwood forest" that the indigenous and early settlers experienced, still blessed with "more species of trees and shrubs than all of Europe."[12]

The Huron River was a significant transportation route for the Native peoples who inhabited its course. So, too, for the pioneers: "The earliest settlers made their way from Detroit up the Huron by flatboat as far as French Landing (Belleville) or Snow's Landing (Rawsonville), striking out overland when they had to with a wagon and a team of oxen."[13] Michigan roads were so bad, in fact, that river transportation was used whenever possible. Many settlers traveled the Huron River to reach their homesteads in Washtenaw County. Moreover, settlers in Ann Arbor and Ypsilanti used the Huron River to raft produce to market in Detroit in the 1820s and 1830s.

Mills to power commercial uses—timber, grain, power—changed the course of the river when installed at Snow's, Ann Arbor, Brighton, Commerce, Delhi, Milford, and Ypsilanti. Such uses dramatically affected others: the spawning runs of herring, muskellunge, sturgeon, and whitefish from Lake Erie were disrupted. A prime example dates from 1910, when the Eastern Michigan Edison Company purchased most of the Van Buren Township land along the Huron River for a hydroelectric plant. The "French Landing" powerhouse and dam were completed in 1924–1925. The dam, largest and last of five constructed on the Huron River, created Belleville Lake. Most of the remaining structures of the town of Rawsonville, founded in 1823, were covered by the lake.

Mill Creek in Dexter is one of the many historic components of the Huron where this juxtaposition of interests has come full circle. Its creekshed is the largest in the Huron watershed, covering 143 square miles. Bisected by I-94, the entire stream network encompasses 226 miles before it empties into the river just north of Dexter. That is where a dam impeded fish upward bound and devastated the natural conditions of this tributary.

Four acres of park land now occupy the former Mill Pond dam impoundment. Dexter received a Michigan Natural Resources Trust Fund Grant and a Waterways Infrastructure Grant in 2009 to develop nonmotorized boat launches, a trail network, natural features, and fishing docks.

On the north side of Main Street behind the fire station, a 2.15-acre park enables strollers to enjoy the creek. A pedestrian bridge carries walkers over the creek and along the pedestrian path through wetland habitat. Trout Unlimited has aided in restoring the fish habitat along this stretch. Five miles of trail along the Huron River links the village to the Huron Clinton Metropolitan Authority Hudson Mills Park.

Recreation is not the only activity available at this locale; the Dexter District Library is perched on an embankment overlooking the meander, and a short walk into town provides numerous shopping and dining options, a number of them in historic structures that date to the nineteenth century.

History reaches back very far here. In October 2015, a farmer whose land abutted one of Mill Creek's branches not far from Chelsea discovered an ancient artifact while digging a catch basin for drainage. Soon realizing the importance of the find, he called for assistance from the University of Michigan. The director of the Museum of Paleontology and team of students conducted an excavation that produced a nearly complete skull, pelvic and rib bones, tusks, and vertebrae. The director rated it as one of ten significant mammoth finds in Michigan's history.

A downtown water landmark anchors Ypsilanti. At the center of town, on the highest point, a mushroom-like tower some 150 feet high rises above the landscape. Completed in 1890, the water tower held a quarter-million gallons of fresh water for the city dwellers, who paid five dollars if they had one tap, an additional two dollars if they had a bathtub—annually. Until 1956, this structure was the only water tower in the system.

Located at the juncture of old Indian trails and the Huron River, the area around Ypsilanti was the camping and burial ground for several Native tribes. In the early 1800s, a trading post was established on the west bank of the Huron, and a group of settlers traveled up the river by boat and settled one mile west. In 1825, Judge Augustus Woodward of Detroit and two local men platted a town. Located on both banks of the Huron at its intersection with the Chicago Road, the town was named to honor the hero of the Greek War of Independence, Demetrius Ypsilanti.

Water and road were not the only means of transportation that the town knew. Michigan's first interurban train, the Ypsilanti and Ann Arbor, began operating in 1890 with a steam engine. Electric power was adopted in 1896, and within a few years a network of interurban railways was built in southern Michigan. The "Ypsi-Ann" was part of the Detroit and Jackson route later extended to Kalamazoo. The last interurban from Ypsilanti sputtered out in 1929, victim of the rise of the automobile.

With its impoundments, the Huron is much changed from its historic look. Still, many have worked to nurture and promote its condition. A primary caretaker of the river is the Huron River Watershed Council (HRWC), which dates back to 1965. Members of the first council included twenty-four units of government. Today, most of the seven counties and sixty-seven townships, villages, and cities within the watershed are members.

The council authors scientific reports to guide decision-making, serving as a common ground where stakeholders can come together to discuss collaboration and coordination supporting the development and passage of statewide legislation that sought to protect water resources. The HRWC played a significant role in securing a state Natural River designation for a portion of the Huron in the 1970s, coordinates several hundred volunteers to monitor the quality of the river, and works with communities to protect the groundwater and surface water that supplies municipal drinking water.

Founded in 1971 by a band of Ann Arbor citizens, the Legacy Land Conservancy is dedicated to the voluntary conservation of locally important land. The conservancy has, after forty-five years, protected more than one hundred individual properties totaling some six thousand acres of conserved lands in the Huron River watershed "that provide safe drinking water, places to play, and vibrant local farms, all right here, where we live."

The Huron has one of the few state-designated Natural River segments in southeast Michigan. The Natural Rivers Act of 1970 authorizes a system of designated and protected Natural Rivers to preserve those with wilderness attributes, others having wild and forested borders, and still others situated in agricultural settings. Sometimes controversial in affected communities because of restrictions placed on development, Natural Rivers designations actually benefit property owners. Michigan State University research shows that property on designated Natural Rivers sells at higher prices and sells more readily than land on nondesignated rivers.

A portion of the Huron has been a "country-scenic" river under the state program since 1977. The protected area includes 27.5 miles of the Huron, plus 10.5 miles of three tributaries. The state defines a country-scenic river as one that is in an "agricultural setting with pastoral borders, some homes, and [is] readily accessible." A more recent designation, attesting to the rebound of the Huron, is its membership in the National Water Trail System, which is administered by the National Park Service. Designated by the US secretary of the interior in 2015, the Huron River Water Trail provides 104 miles of paddling. System membership qualifies the river's advocates and caretakers for technical and funding assistance. The Park Service says water trails "are recreational routes on waterways with a network of public access points supported by broad-based community partnerships. Water trails provide both conservation and recreational opportunities."[14]

Early in the twentieth century the Huron spawned a cottage industry forgotten today: shell-fishing. "The Huron River was one of a half-dozen rivers in southern Michigan which produced enough freshwater mussels, or clams, to nurture a significant but brief industry in the early 1900s."[15] These mussels were used to make pearl buttons. Their names are evocative: black sand shell, hickory nut, maple-leaf, mucket, pigtoe, pimple-back, pocketbook, three-ridge. Also exploited for shells were the St. Clair River, Lake St. Clair, and Detroit River. The latter had one of the greatest varieties of freshwater mussels in the entire Great Lakes. A once-thriving industry collapsed with overharvesting and degradation of the freshwater beds where the organism made its home.

Hull's Trace

When the United States declared war against Great Britain in June 1812, General William Hull ordered the construction of a military road between

Fort Detroit and points south. The road was renamed the "Great Military Road" and underwent improvements after the War of 1812, becoming one of the first of a national system of military roads ordered by Congress and later administered under the secretary of war.

The road has many identities along its lengthy route: Jefferson in Detroit and downriver; Biddle in Wyandotte, connoting that community's early settler; the US Turnpike, North Dixie Highway, Kentucky Avenue, and others in Monroe County. As an early road authorized by the US government in Michigan, it is of historical interest. The construction of a "corduroy road" involved some complexity:

> The first step in the construction of a road was the survey of its route. After this was accomplished, contracts were let to an enterprising citizen, who in turn hired a gang of men to do the work. Trees were cut as low to the ground as possible; stumps and exposed roots remained. Because of the density of the forests, little sunlight fell on the road and consequently mudholes and puddles usually never dried out. In such cases, brush and logs were thrown over the wet areas forming a corduroy road.[16]

It's a natural assumption that all vestiges of such routes have long disappeared. Amazingly, in 2000 low water levels in the Huron River revealed a quarter mile of the old corduroy road, lying three to six feet beneath Jefferson Avenue. Axe marks were visible on some of the logs. This rare example of a surviving corduroy road is listed in the National Register of Historic Places. It is the only known log remnant of the first military and federal road in Michigan.

A Michigan historical marker stands near the site where Jefferson and Harbin roads meet. To view the remnants, one must travel on Harbin west, or approach the embankment under Jefferson from the west on the water. The logs have long been submerged due to the surrounding water levels. The site is now a unit of the River Raisin National Battlefield Park.

The Detroit River International Wildlife Refuge has a cooperative management agreement with U.S. Silica for conservation of approximately one hundred acres of wetlands at the mouth of the Huron River adjacent to Hull's Trace. The National Park Service has acquired an old public access site at the mouth from Wayne County. The Park Service will interpret history and the US Fish and Wildlife Service will interpret conservation there, in partnership with U.S. Silica.

Pointe Mouillee

Here, a land/waterscape mimics the original shoreline of this corner of Lake Erie. The Huron once met the Great Lakes "in a vast delta of marshes, formed in a process of give-and-take with" Erie.[17] This is where the French roots have resurfaced in the renewal of Pointe Mouillee, a rich habitat for waterfowl and game.

Northeast lower Michigan has marketed itself as the "Sunrise Side" of the state, inviting tourists and visitors to watch the dawn on Lake Huron. The same opportunity exists at Pointe Mouillee, where the sun comes up every morning facing the western shore of Lake Erie as it has for thousands of years. This State Game Area consists of over four thousand acres of freshwater marsh near the mouth of the Huron River. Pointe Mouillee hosts one of the oldest waterfowl festivals in the nation. It is also North America's largest freshwater marsh restoration project.

The name ("wet point") comes from French fur traders in the seventeenth century. It is one of the most important waterfowl habitats in Michigan. Hunting and bird-watching go hand in hand here, reflecting the modern foundation for the park. In 1875, a group of local hunters acquired some two thousand acres for the Pointe Mouillee Shooting Club. The state established the public game area beginning in 1945 with the acquisition of twenty-six hundred acres.

The fluctuating water levels of Lake Erie had eroded a protective barrier island, inundating some wetlands. Restoration began in the early 1980s when the US Army Corps of Engineers sought a disposal site for contaminated dredge material. A seven-hundred-acre mound, fourteen hundred feet wide and nearly four miles in length, was built up offshore roughly in the same shape of the original barrier island. The end result of this decision-making and investment: "a regenerated marsh with thriving wetlands, marshes, and river bayous."[18]

Before Monroe

The mouth of Swan Creek is south of Pointe Mouillee. The Michigan Water Trails website describes "an easy paddle from Swan Creek launch to Lake Erie and back."

On the north side of the creek's mouth is Estral Beach, a town incorporated in 1925. The village hosts an annual Swan Creek cleanup to tidy the environment while raising money (in 2016) for village maintenance garage improvements. To the immediate south is the DTE Energy Fermi nuclear power generating facility. The latter was located on the shore of Lake Erie for easy access to fresh water for cooling. More than six hundred acres of the site became part of the Detroit River International Wildlife Refuge in 2003.

Pointe Aux Peaux is the next geographic feature along the Erie lakeshore. French for "point of skins," the name associated the site with Native history and culture. The Native peoples had used the location to dry their pelts on the flat rocks adjoining the lake. In 1867, Joseph M. Sterling and several other Monroe investors bought twenty-five acres here to establish a vineyard and winery on Lake Erie. After Sterling's death in 1891, the winery building was converted into a home. It was known thereafter locally as the Stone House. Since then a home incorporating the original building inside has been fashioned. A nearby state wildlife area stretches south through mudflats into Brest Bay.

Settled by the French around 1810, "Brest" evoked one of the great seaports of their native land. Located on the lake road between Ohio and Detroit, it inspired great plans in the minds of some Monroe County investors. It was to be the port for the Gibraltar & Flat Rock Company, a scheme that failed. Another brainstorm was the incorporation of the Brest Bank here in September 1837. One of the many wildcat money institutions that sprang up under an ill-advised act of the legislature, the bank was undercapitalized and overpapered and its hard assets woefully inadequate. A colorful account of an encounter by a visitor reveals the hard story:

A trip in the fall of 1838, on horseback, discovered the palaces of "rag barons" to consist of a very small hotel, a store, and a bank building, costing $1,711. There were also included in this category hundreds of city lots for sale in *currency of any kind.* The population was myriads, consisting, unfortunately, of musquitos. Large fires were built about the tavern to determine whether the guests should eat or be eaten, and whether the hum of the busy and musical denizens should disturb their sleep. They were the natural guardians of the untold gold that the bank vaults were supposed to contain. No one visited that place twice in pursuit of gold or a gold mine. At this date the city lots are not sold, and but for its banking history the city would be unknown.[19]

Situated between the larger Huron River and the River Raisin watersheds, the Stony Creek watershed is long and narrow, more than thirty miles in length and eight miles wide. It reaches north of Milan and US-23 and touches the southern boundaries of Ann Arbor and Ypsilanti. For much of its length a road of the same name parallels its course. A quarter of the watershed is forested or shrubbery, another quarter grassland. Wetlands make up less than 3 percent of the watershed.

Sterling State Park

This is the only state park on Lake Erie. Named for William C. Sterling, a lumber baron who loved to go duck hunting amid the marshes of western Lake Erie's Michigan shore, the park consists of thirteen hundred acres of land, a sandy beach, and other amenities. Sterling was a principal factor in founding of the Monroe Marsh Club in 1880. A premier yachtsman, he had varying business and sporting interests. His was one of the pioneer families of the county.[20] Upon his death in 1924, the Monroe Piers Land Company donated acreage to the state for a park named in honor of the local leader.[21]

Decades of pollution resulting from the discharges of the River Raisin and the Detroit River tainted the waters off Sterling State Park in the mid-twentieth century. Swimming in the lake was strongly discouraged with warning signs. But more protective pollution laws rehabilitated those waters.

In 2001, Sterling State Park was made the southern border of the Detroit River International Wildlife Refuge, enabling federal funding for a $12 million renovation. The park was closed, redesigned, and reopened with miles of wetland walking paths open to the public in an area that had been closed since the early 1900s. The Department of Natural Resources sought to recreate acres of emergent and submergent Great Lakes marsh and lake-plain prairie, and to repair dikes and install water control for 310 acres of marsh.

Monroe

Monroe County is the only Michigan county on the western shore of Lake Erie. The original identity of its namesake city, Frenchtown, signifies its non-American origin.

The city of Monroe is the historic heart of the county. Here is extensive locally sponsored historical signage, a War of 1812 national battlefield park, and evidence that the fresh waters of the river and lake and region combined to produce a wealth of human heritage.

An iconic attraction is the Trading Post complex. Designed to represent a French pioneer homestead along the River Raisin, the main building, raised in 1789 by Utreau Navarre, is the oldest wooden residence still standing in

Michigan. It is also the most complete example of French-Canadian "piece-sur-piece" construction in the Old Northwest. Other buildings include an 1810 cookhouse and a replica 1790s French-Canadian style barn.

Monroe suffered one great historical disappointment. In 1817, James Monroe took a great western tour to inspect military facilities along the Canadian border, among other purposes, and Monroe prepared itself for the first-ever visit to Michigan of a US president. The president crossed Lake Erie to Detroit in late August and stayed in the city for five days. Concluding his sojourn, he departed for Sandusky. Historical records attest that he bypassed the city bearing his name, perhaps a result of fatigue from his lengthy travels.[22]

Monroe was also the site of several lighthouses to aid in water navigation. In May 1828, the federal government authorized construction of a structure at Otter Creek Point south of town. The mouth of the River Raisin was shallow as its waters traveled through marshes and sandbars. Early passenger and cargo traffic docked in LaPlaisance Bay and relied on wagons and horse-drawn railroad cars to reach Monroe. Westerly winds often lowered the lake level, making the entrance navigable only by small craft.

In 1834, Monroe's leaders petitioned Congress for improvements at the mouth of the River Raisin to enable larger ships to enter the river and exit it into Lake Erie. A canal one hundred feet wide, four thousand feet long, and twelve feet deep was authorized and pursued, creating a Monroe Harbor approximately four miles north of the Otter Creek Lighthouse. A new lighthouse was completed in 1849 at the new harbor, and the Otter Creek Lighthouse was decommissioned the same year and dismantled.

By the 1890s, the Monroe waterfront attracted a crush of summer visitors. Passenger vessels like the 125-foot side-wheeled steamer *Jeanie* made trips daily between Monroe and Toledo. The Monroe Piers Hotel Company was formed in 1895, and the twenty-five-room Hotel Lotus opened that summer on the beach north of the lighthouse. Word about the resort hotel spread, prompting excursioners to come from Canada, Cleveland, Detroit, Sandusky, and Toledo. Trolley cars traveled from downtown Monroe along the north side of the river to the waterfront pier, and in 1905 some seventy thousand passengers were carried on the "Beach Line" trolley.

In 1916, an automated gaslight system was installed on a steel skeleton structure on the pier, and the lighthouse was abandoned. In 1922, the US government sold the structure, and soon thereafter it was dismantled. Only traces of these lighthouses remain to tell the story of how ships formerly depended on these beacons of safety.

In place of the trolley line, a River Raisin Heritage Trail is connecting downtown Monroe to the River Raisin National Battlefield Visitor Center and on to Sterling State Park.[23] The trail will run by some of Monroe's oldest and most elegant homes. In addition, a ten-foot wide river walk accompanies much of the waterway.

In front of the Dorsch Memorial Library on East First Street remains one of "Michigan's most famous and historic trees." The library is the former home of and is named for Dr. Edward Dorsch, a prominent physician of the 1860s who came to America "seeking freedom from political tyranny." He planted a ginkgo seedling in the front lawn here after receiving it as a gift from the Chinese ambassador. He was something of a nature lover, and "among his many horiticultural [sic] efforts was the importation of lotus seeds which he planted in marshes near his Monroe home." He was a presidential elector in the 1860 election and served the country by providing physical exams and care to the Monroe volunteer soldiers during the Civil War. One hundred fifty years later, the tree stands tall in front of the library.[24]

The two plants have been used to provide entertainment for Monroe residents. "From high atop the Benesh Building in beautiful downtown Monroe," says the introduction to *The Lotus Ginkgo Show*, a weekly parody talk show on Monroe public access cable television. The program host is "a cynical, self-loathing, irreverent fictional character named Lotus Ginkgo."

The River Raisin National Battlefield Park was established in 2009 as the 393rd unit of the National Park Service. It is the only national battlefield park associated with the War of 1812. The battle was the costliest defeat of the war for the Americans, resulting in between 300 and 400 Americans killed and approximately 560 wounded or captured at the hands of the British and Native American allies. The loss, and the subsequent slaughter of around 100 American wounded, became a rallying cry for the Americans.

The locally run visitor center will eventually be replaced by one more consistent with the federal government style; the park has already grown since its establishment thanks to donations of land. Attendance has already exceeded expectations. In 2016, more than 202,000 people from twenty nations and forty-nine states visited.[25]

Originally dubbed Nummaspee, or River of Sturgeon by Native Americans, the River Raisin derives its current name from plentiful grapes that the French noted on its banks. It drains a watershed approximately the size of the state of Rhode Island. The river is now recovering from abuse and neglect that left it degraded enough to be another designated Great Lakes area of concern. Bottom sediments in the lower 2.6 miles of the river, a half mile out into Lake Erie and adjacent areas close to shore north and south one mile had been heavily contaminated with toxic PCBs, a result of past industrial discharges. A $30 million cleanup was planned in the summer of 2016 to remove a significant share of the toxic riverbed.

Even more exciting to the community was the removal of dams, allowing fish passage on the lower twenty-three miles of the river after seventy years of obstruction. Coupled with improved water quality, this opened the door for the potential return of the iconic lake sturgeon, once known to spawn in the Raisin. Lake sturgeon can live over a century and grow to lengths of seven feet or more. The river also provides habitat for walleye, smallmouth bass, northern pike, and muskie.

Bald eagles can be seen along the river's banks, but the biggest local congregation of America's symbol can be found in winter months at the DTE power plant on Lake Erie. The thermal discharge from the plant typically preserves open water when all else is frozen, making the spot an ideal fishing ground for the eagles.

Although all surface water in southeast Michigan discharges to Lake Erie, the Raisin plays an especially significant role in Erie's health. Plagued by algae blooms since the late 1990s, the western basin of Erie receives an excess of phosphorus from farm animal waste and chemical fertilizer, along with runoff from city streets and lawns.

About 18 percent of the land in the western Lake Erie basin lies within Michigan, the Raisin being the largest Michigan tributary emptying into the lake. Intensive farming characterizes much of the Raisin's watershed, as is true of the Indiana and Ohio land that drains into western Lake Erie. More frequent and intense rainstorms during the critical spring planting period, a manifestation of climate change, drive phosphorus from animal waste and commercial fertilizers just applied into waterways leading to Erie.

Southeast Michigan philanthropy is trying to foster solutions. The Fred A. and Barbara M. Erb Family Foundation provided $480,000 over three years to the Michigan Association of Conservation Districts (MACD) to spur farmers to adopt conservation practices to protect water quality in Michigan's portion of the Erie Basin.[26] The project is also intended to strengthen farmer leadership to encourage neighbor action. MACD, the River Raisin Watershed Council, the Lenawee Conservation District, and the Michigan Department of Agriculture and Rural Development were project partners.

The Journey Ends

The final leg of the passage through the heart of the lakes begins at Luna Pier. The municipality is a twentieth-century invention, having incorporated in 1963.

Michigan is the place where one can find all sorts of pleasant peninsulas. Besides the Upper and Lower, there are plenty more: Garden, Keweenaw, Leelanau, Old Mission. None is more evocative than the "Lost Peninsula." Isolated, inaccessible from the rest of mainland Michigan, hidden, the approximately 240 acres of land is cut off from its state by a redrawn border. Ohio and Michigan contended, when the latter was seeking statehood in 1835–1837, over where their mutual boundary should be located. Ohio argued for a boundary north of Toledo in order to secure the port of Maumee Bay. Michigan pointed to ironclad documents that drew the line south of the Maumee River. Ohio prevailed since it had full representation in Congress, while Michigan, as a territory, did not. The end result was to benefit Michigan, since it gained the western half of the Upper Peninsula in the bargain. And the Lost Peninsula.[27]

The tiny finger of land, with its water-based street names—Edgewater, Bay, Peninsula—can be reached from Michigan directly only over water. Fresh water. Water that has seen pollution, disrespect and disinvestment— and then recovery.

But what lies ahead for southeast Michigan's fresh water?

A Water Legacy

Because of the abundance of lakes, rivers, woods, and shoreline that sur-
rounds us, those of us fortunate enough to live in Michigan have a special
duty to preserve our natural heritage.

—William Clay Ford Jr.

n 2017, a half-century after pollution of the Detroit River and its tributaries
shamed America and galvanized public demand for an environmental
cleanup, the times are beginning to change again. A trip down the river
tells a story profoundly different from the tale of dystopian decay that the
world associated with Detroit and the region. Signs of hope are multiplying.
Recreationalists ply the river as oceangoing vessels pass. Businesses in search
of plentiful clean water—and associated quality of life for their employees—
are locating here. Investment has returned to the shoreline.

The abundance of natural resources was the foundation of the original
economic prosperity of southern Michigan.[1] It is providing benefits again,

supporting recovery from the Great Recession that began in 2008. That near-depression hammered at the state's well-being and pushed the city of Detroit, already teetering, into bankruptcy. Over a decade after that downturn began, Michigan has come back a long way, by all indices. It has seen significant employment growth and has its highest personal income ever, when adjusted for inflation.

There is something else to build on. The Michigan ethic of conservation is embedded in its constitution.

> The conservation and development of the natural resources of the state are hereby declared to be of paramount public concern in the interest of the health, safety and general welfare of the people. The legislature shall provide for the protection of the air, water and other natural resources of the state from pollution, impairment and destruction.[2]

Business leaders now embrace sustainable use and conservation of resources. A 2015 "Michigan Natural Resources Business Plan" sought to leverage the state's assets to make Michigan a top-ten state for jobs, personal income, and a healthy economy. Its freshwater assets stood front and center in the vision:

> Michigan is blessed with abundant and diverse natural resources, which are a significant part of the state's culture, history, identity, and economy. Our natural resources attract visitors, residents, and businesses to the state. . . . We use natural resources, particularly water, as part of the process for many of our other critical industries, including Michigan's manufacturing and energy sectors. Water is also key to our tourism and recreation economies.

The plan recognized that the academic and business research and development sectors provided a strong base of intellectual resources that fueled innovation and contributed to the state's potential to capitalize on its natural resource economy. It also looked to the longer term, where "Michigan is also uniquely situated to benefit economically from its freshwater resources in several respects, including research and development, as a key enabler of other industries (e.g., agriculture and manufacturing), and as a continued part of making Michigan an attractive place to live and do business."[3]

Other planning and vision documents place water near the top of the list of lures for economic development. A 2014 "green infrastructure" vision prepared by the Southeast Michigan Council of Governments (SEMCOG) focused on the region's parks, lakes, wetlands, trees, constructed green roofs, bioswales, and rain gardens. SEMCOG tallied in the region more than 180,000 acres of public parks, over 900,000 acres of trees, and the largest coastal wetland system in the Great Lakes.

"Green infrastructure is increasingly being recognized for its contribution not only to environmental quality, but also to placemaking, economic values, and healthy communities—things that are vitally important to individual communities and the region," the vision document said. "Additionally, green infrastructure can be used to protect and restore many of the region's jewels—inland lakes and streams—as well as the Great Lakes from Lake Huron through the St. Clair River, Lake St. Clair, and Detroit River to Lake Erie. These waterways are nationally recognized and bring billions annually to Michigan's economy." The vision called for the entire regional green infrastructure network to be managed as a system.

SEMCOG's February 2016 economic development strategy for the region also underscored the region's abundance of water resources—one hundred thousand acres of it—and its place as a link between the upper and lower Great Lakes. It suggested the region's governments and other institutions should promote and support activities along area waterways, including blue economy plans and waterfront redevelopment. The reference to a blue economy was not casual. The phrase was at the center of much economic thinking. John Austin, author of a 2013 white paper on the subject and director of the Michigan Economic Center, defined "blue economy" as the contribution Michigan's natural water assets, emerging water education and research centers, and technology-based businesses make to jobs and economic development benefits. He estimated the economic impact in Michigan of water-based economic activity at nearly one million jobs and $60 billion annually.

Austin listed the state's water-related economic benefits:

- Shipping, freight/commercial traffic and warehousing contributed over 65,000 Michigan jobs and $3.3 billion in annual wages.
- 660,000 jobs and $49 billion in annual wages were linked to water-dependent farming, manufacturing, mining, and energy production.
- Coastal tourism from birding to beach visits was responsible for 57,000 jobs and $955 million in earnings every year.

In addition, there were over 350 emerging water-technology-based firms in Michigan, moving into a global market for water cleaning, conservation, restoration, monitoring, infrastructure-building, and engineering.

Austin observed that Michigan could not afford simply to contemplate a blue economy; a global race for leadership was on. In the Great Lakes region alone, Milwaukee, Cleveland, Buffalo, and Ontario were all developing blue economy initiatives. "Michigan needs to catch-up and leapfrog states and communities vying for the prize of water technology, research and education leadership, and who are marketing their water-based natural assets and sustainability/lifestyle 'brand,'" Austin said.

What would it really mean for southeast Michigan to become a freshwater hub of research and development? Milwaukee offers some clues—and illustrates the opportunity to community leaders of the Detroit metropolis. Downtown Milwaukee's redevelopment is often cited as a model, including apartments with views of the Milwaukee River, an accessible Lake Michigan waterfront, and a municipal sewer system praised for conserving water. Nothing about these is alien to southeast Michigan. What in fact was one of the differences?

A noticeable distinction is that Milwaukee has one of only three graduate-level studies in freshwater sciences in the world, part of the University of Wisconsin–Milwaukee. The UW-M School of Freshwater Sciences offers this rationale for being:

> Freshwater is fundamental to the prosperity of our communities. Clean freshwater systems lead to a better environment, economy, and quality of life. Milwaukee's citizens interact directly and indirectly with their Freshwater river systems and lake on a daily basis. We rely on our fresh-tasting drinking water, the riverside walkways of our downtown economic hub, and free-access recreational beaches for a higher quality of life.
>
> The School of Freshwater Sciences' students, research faculty, and staff generate cutting-edge research that improves the lives of Milwaukeeans and can impact urban dwellers across the nation.

The school harbors twenty-one research laboratories. Their capabilities range from microbiology and genomics to aquaculture and groundwater, result in revolutionary research collaborations. The school formed on-site partnerships with public agencies involved in freshwater protection, including the University of Wisconsin Sea Grant, Wisconsin Department of Natural Resources and U.S. Department of Agriculture, and the US Environmental Protection Agency's Lake Guardian vessel.

So well recognized is the school that in 2014–2015 delegations from South Korea, China, Brazil, and other countries visited its headquarters on Freshwater Way, near the banks of the Menomonee River, a walking trail, and the Harley-Davidson Museum. The strategic placement of a state-of-the-art university freshwater research facility at the hub of projects along a reawakening urban waterfront offers one of several examples to southeast Michigan.

The higher-education capability certainly exists here. The University Research Corridor, an alliance among Michigan State University, the University of Michigan, and Wayne State University, seeks to transform, strengthen and diversify the state's economy. In 2016, the three institutions together drew nearly $2 billion in federal academic research funding to Michigan, the overwhelming majority of the total coming into the state. URC universities announced an average of one new invention every day over the previous five years. These discoveries led to more than five hundred license agreements for new technologies and systems. The three schools drew students from all over the world; in early 2016 their combined enrollment exceeded 120,000 men and women, more than could fit into Michigan Stadium in Ann Arbor on a crisp fall football day. The opportunity for invention and genius was unprecedented.

The region's higher-education resources play a major part in a detailed blueprint for southeast Michigan's emergence as a global freshwater hub. Developed by Austin with advice from economists, business leaders, and others, the plan calls for the following components:

- *A World Freshwater Innovation Center in Detroit.* To promote local, Great Lakes, and global freshwater innovation, universities, corporations, and philanthropists would organize and fund a Michigan equivalent of the Scripps Institute for Freshwater Innovation, promoting water research, education, development, and commercialization of new ideas and technologies.
- *Centers of excellence at Michigan's water education and research centers.* Michigan has nine university water research and education centers, and eighteen community colleges with significant water education programming. The footprint and growth of these programs would be expanded by a "water consortium" of higher-education institutions, supported by private and public entities, to (1) develop a coordinated curriculum around water that takes advantage of geographic location and (2) develop a network of research practitioners to solve key problems.
- *A Pure Michigan Water Technology Innovation Fund.* Michigan would create a new blue economy catalyst organization similar in purpose to what Milwaukee developed through its Water Council to commercialize new water technology products and develop new firms.

- *A business-led Blue Business Council to champion the blue economy.*
  A business-led Blue Business Council of Michigan water technology
  product and service firms could provide important functions to grow
  the blue economy.

These initiatives offer the promise of a new age of prosperity in southeast
Michigan, an age that would also provide a service to all of humanity. But
the state can demonstrate leadership only if it takes care of its own business,
and that is by no means assured.

Chronic underfunding of public drinking water and wastewater systems—exacerbated by elected officials fearful of or in partnership with
antitax forces—is putting Michigan's clean water at risk. A study released
in 2016 estimated that annual Michigan community public investment
in drinking water systems was about $450 million, short by between $284
million and $563 million of the amount needed to provide safe drinking
water. Sewage system needs were likely even greater. Michigan cities reported
$2.14 billion in sewer infrastructure needs.[4] The state's leading public officials
and taxpayers will have to face the fact.

The state and municipalities will also have to maintain or strengthen
all of the protections put in place for Michigan's water since the 1970s:
the Natural Rivers program protecting a portion of the Huron River; the
wetlands law sustaining this dwindling but life-giving, pollution-filtering
resource; the laws and rules limiting both sewage and toxic chemicals. To
serve as the freshwater hub of North America, southeast Michigan must
lead by example.

Continued environmental restoration is also necessary. The Obama administration's $2 billion Great Lakes Restoration Initiative gave a substantial
boost to southeast Michigan's water resources. Funding went a long way to
heal impairments at the region's areas of concern—the St. Clair, Clinton,
Detroit, and Rouge Rivers and River Raisin—support wetland restoration
at Pointe aux Peaux and Humbug Marsh, control invasive phragmites at
the St. Clair Flats, and install fish passage structures on the Raisin. There is

no assurance that federal funding under subsequent administrations will continue, leaving it to the state and municipalities to find resources.

In some ways, the question facing southeast Michigan is an old one. Is its lengthy freshwater shore awash with numerous rivers and streams to be exploited, taken for granted, or nurtured? More than seven decades ago, Michigan's conservation department asked this very question, one that applies to all humanity.

> In our hours of ease lakes and streams invite boating, bathing, hunting, fishing; in the winter time frozen waters give us skating, skiing, tobogganing. What would a landscape be like without waters?
>
> As the forests were believed inexhaustible, so now water resources are believed to be never-failing. . . .
>
> The State's second industry, its tourist and resort business, depends, among other things, upon the highest quality of our natural waters.[5]

The freshwater attributes were even then the key to the future:

> With its fascinating open waters, lush freshwater wetlands along the coast, tallgrass prairie and savanna ecosystems near the shoreline, and woodlands that once existed across much of its inland area, the Lake Huron to Lake Erie Corridor is a uniquely beautiful part of Earth. What happens in this region can have an impact on other parts of the world.[6]

Watershed management has now become a major actor in the drama of a potential transition for southeast Michigan into a world-class water hub. Protection of the resource represents one of "the necessary building blocks to restore and maintain" southeast Michigan's vitality.[7]

Riverfronts have changed. No longer is the Detroit shore dominated by smokestacks and waste piles. The city has turned its face to the river again, as have residents, users, patrons of the Huron, the Raisin, and the Rouge flowing into Lake Erie, and the Clinton and the Black into Lake St. Clair.

Major changes are coming to the Detroit River International Wildlife Refuge. Improvements planned for the area are aimed at increasing visitation. Over $3 million was raised to construct a structure stretching 740 feet into the Detroit River featuring a fishing pier and floating dock for the Great Lakes School Ship. The latter will provide mooring for the Michigan Sea Grant educational program boat. Anglers without access to a boat will be able to fish for competition-size walleye in the depths of the river because of the access provided by the length of the pier. Additional amenities include three wildlife observation decks, a kayak launch/landing, an environmental education shelter, 2.5 miles of trails, and a twelve-thousand-square-foot Gold LEED-certified visitor center, completed in spring 2019.

When completed, the former brownfield will decisively demonstrate southeast Michigan's transformation. It was not an overnight phenomenon.

Other well-meaning persons of vision called for "dreaming big—no, huge—in Detroit." Perhaps an attraction, like converting the old New York Central train station into the world's largest children's museum, or a giant Model T near the forthcoming New International Crossing bridge.[8] Of course, the Gordie Howe span might itself serve this purpose if properly designed. The vigorous partnership between Ontario and Michigan to build the bridge demonstrates powerfully the region's premier position as a strategic logistics hub.

Perhaps, if an imaginative plan is adopted, visitors to southeast Michigan will encounter—on their way in from Metro Airport, or crossing into the state from Ohio, or along the I-94 corridor—a sign welcoming them to the Freshwater Heart of North America. This would replace a blight of burned-out buildings.

Thinking even bigger, leaders have the chance to embrace an initiative to create a regional amenity and a globally significant freshwater landmark. The Huron-to-Erie corridor could become the site of the first national greenway within the National Park system.

That trails were a significant development in the history of southeast Michigan is due in no small measure to the Community Foundation for

A Thriving Home for Fresh Water and Fresh Ideas

To function and flourish as the heart of the Great Lakes, rather than merely happening to be at the heart of the Great Lakes, southeast Michigan needs to take several initiatives:

- Detroit prospers as the hub of growing global trade for the Great Lakes and the United States and Canada (symbolized by the new Gordie Howe International Bridge and improved international truck, rail, port, and intermodal facilities in Detroit and Port Huron).
- Southeast Michigan becomes the thriving home for Great Lakes research and fresh ideas, invention and innovation (building on the New Economy Initiative of the Community Foundation of Southeast Michigan, a strategy working to build an inclusive network of support for entrepreneurs and small businesses in southeast Michigan), major research universities, and corporate R & D.
- Governments invest in clean drinking water infrastructure so that lead and other contaminants never again threaten the health and safety of families, firms, and communities anywhere in this freshwater capital.
- An Emerald Arc forms on the northern and western border of southeast Michigan, where ten great rivers originate, and a next generation of sustainable farming spreads to free the downstream waters from the nitrogen-phosphate fertilizer runoff and algae blooms that befoul Lakes Huron, St. Clair, and Erie and threaten our drinking water.
- Detroit and southeast Michigan reclaim through green infrastructure the natural filters, flood controls, wetlands, and outdoor spaces of this unique confluence of ten river watersheds that recharge three Great Lakes.

- The growing network of greenways crisscrossing the region provides access for all residents and visitors to the great outdoors, our rivers, lakes, and streams, and healthy living.
- The Detroit–Great Lakes National Greenway is authorized as the first urban linear national park by extending the Detroit RiverWalk all the way northeast to Lake Huron and south to Lake Erie; linked greenways run up all of the major tributaries so that all the communities along the way—led by Detroit—can become river towns once again; and southeast Michigan becomes the nation's leader for walking, peddling, paddling, and outdoor recreation.
- Local Citizen Conservation Corps engage thousands of volunteers in renewing and restoring our natural assets and ensuring that Detroit and southeast Michigan become a thriving a home for fresh water and fresh ideas and reclaim their destiny as the heart of the Great Lakes.

Southeast Michigan. In 2001, the foundation launched the Southeast Michigan GreenWays Initiative "to create opportunities for collaboration and shared environmental awareness and appreciation by the residents of the seven-county region [Thus] began a five-year initiative as a comprehensive effort to expand and enhance our region's natural landscape."[9]

As of the fall of 2016, the GreenWays Initiative had led to one hundred miles of connected greenways involving more than eighty municipalities across southeast Michigan. $33 million dollars in foundation and private contributions had leveraged $125 million of matching investments from government and other sources. Communities all over the region were seeing benefits from the Flat Rock Connector, Dequindre Cut, Conner Creek/Milibank Greenway, Lyndon Greenway, Rouge River Gateway Greenway, Midtown Loop Greenway, Downriver Linked Greenways, and the Border to Border Trail on the Huron River.

An intangible but profoundly meaningful result of the initiative was a culture of civic cooperation. More than fifteen hundred people attended meetings organized by the foundation to explore the idea of connecting communities, fostering cooperation, and stimulating greenway construction.

Tom Woiwode, director of the GreenWays Initiative, explains that greenways intersect with healthier communities in three ways. "The first has to do with changing the landscape and our relationship to our environment. A greener landscape creates a healthier, more vibrant environment and community; and a cleaner community generates a number of benefits, including cleaner air—thus, less asthma, healthier people, aesthetically pleasing surroundings, which creates a more positive attitude toward one's community, and a greater interest in community."

The second, Woiwode says, builds on the first, and "it addresses the water issue directly—greenways and a greener landscape help manage water more effectively, thus reducing the need for investment in gray infrastructure while providing a system that helps cleanse the water naturally. The third has to do with the use of greenways. The more people are out and exercising, the healthier we are as a society, thus reducing the cost of health care and making everyone much happier."[10] But there is much more to come.

The long-range vision for southeast Michigan greenways includes a more than one-hundred-mile coastal link from Port Huron to Monroe—a breathtaking dream of national significance. It would merit designation as the first national greenway. A unit in the National Park system but administered in cooperation with the state and participating municipalities, the Greenway could become a globally known attraction, an economic magnet, and a connection between citizens and their water resources, reinforcing the public's affinity for and stewardship of the environment.

All the idea lacks is a champion.

As a changing climate evaporates water from former boom lands in America's Sunbelt, southeast Michigan can lead the way in securing the world's epicenter of fresh water for future generations. Becoming the hub of the Great Lakes and the global capital for fresh water and fresh ideas would convert what some still see as a rust belt region abandoned and dilapidated into a premier center for economic vitality and a sterling quality of life.

But serious questions persist. Will something like the plan set forth by Austin attract the support of southeast Michigan's leaders? Can the region outgrow old divisions and organize itself to become a water sustainability research, demonstration, and stewardship capital? Will there be investment sufficient to preserve, protect, and defend the region's key asset: unhindered access to humanity's most critical natural and cultural resource? This is a monumentally important question. Perhaps most importantly, is there civic leadership to put this all together?

The answers aren't difficult to find. They reside within the people of southeast Michigan.

The waters of southeast Michigan are stunning. Reach into the funneling Lake Huron on the beach at Fort Gratiot Lighthouse as it prepares for its ninety-mile journey to Erie. Stand on the observation deck at Humbug Marsh, greeting the breeze of a southwestern wind that speaks more of the promise of the next spring than of a last gasp of autumn. Imagine on the Detroit RiverWalk how Native peoples camped here, fugitives from enslavement first gazed into freedom here, and the hope of a great American city took flight here.

"If there is magic on this planet, it is contained in water," Loren Eiseley said. To achieve greatness again, southeast Michigan need only recognize that magic, and make it work for the common good.

NOTES

Preface

1. Wayne Grady, *The Great Lakes: The Natural History of a Changing Region* (Vancouver, BC: Greystone Books, 2007), 9.

2. Daniel Howes, "Is Failure Manufactured Too Often in Michigan?" *Detroit News*, February 16, 2016.

Chapter 2. The Headwaters

1. Doner, a Port Huron native, renamed the St. Clair River as the Blue in her novel. See *Blue River* (Garden City, NY: Doubleday, 1946).

2. Northwest Ordinance, July 13, 1787, www.loc.gov.

3. Bruce Catton, *Michigan: A Bicentennial History* (New York: W.W. Norton, 1976), 20–21, 24.

4. https://www.cmich.edu/library/clarke/ResearchResources/Michigan_Material_Local/Detroit_Pre_statehood_Descriptions/Entries_by_Date/Pages/1702-Antoine-Laumet-De-Lemothe-Cadillac.aspx.

5. Detroit Water and Sewerage Department, "Remembering Those Who Died," http://www.dwsd.org/downloads_n/about_dwsd/history/explosion.pdf.

6. "In Michigan History: Deadly Lake Huron Tunnel Explostion," *Detroit News*, September 17, 2016.

7. In addition to the Blue Water Bridges Excursion discussed here, the Blueways of St. Clair includes the first National Water Trail in Michigan, the 10.2-mile Island Loop. The trail includes segments of the Black River, the Black River Canal, Lake Huron, and the St. Clair River. The National Water Trails System is intended to yoke existing and new water trails into a national network.

8. The Blueways of St. Clair, http://www.bluewaysofstclair.org.

9. In 1769, the British built Fort Sinclair at the mouth of the Black River in modern-day Port Huron. That spot was chosen "so that the British canoes and ships could be protected from the naval forces that were posted between Lake St. Clair and Lake Huron." *Michigan History*, "Fort Sinclair Part 2," http://michiganhistory.leadr.msu.edu/fort-sinclair-part-2/.

10. William A. Jenks, "Fort Gratiot and Its Builder Gen. Charles Gratiot," *Michigan History Magazine* 4 (1920): 145.

11. Fred Landon, *Lake Huron* (Indianapolis: Bobbs-Merrill, 1944), 100.

12. Ibid., 149.

13. Ibid., 149, 151.

14. Ibid., 100.

15. Among impaired uses that remained were restrictions on fish and wildlife consumption, loss of habitat, and restrictions on drinking water consumption.

16. Http://www.cityofmarysvillemi.com/about-us/museum/history-of-marysville.

17. Bureau of History, *Pathways to Michigan's Black Heritage* (Lansing: Michigan Department of State, 1988), 11.

18. Walter Romig, *Michigan Place Names: The History of the Founding and the Naming of More Than Five Thousand Past and Present Michigan Communities* (Detroit: Wayne State University Press, 1986), 352.

19. Ibid., 17.

20. "Chris Smith and Gar Wood Now Fixtures in Algonac City Park," *The Voice*, July 6, 2010, http://www.voicenews.com/articles/2010/07/06/news/doc4c2b95d7143cb545760472.txt.

21. Recognizing the natural bounty of the flats, the Michigan Legislature in 1913 authorized the state to make rules to provide for the preservation and use of the paramount right of navigation, hunting, and fishing covering the entire St. Clair Flats area.

22. *Explore Our Natural World: A Biodiversity Atlas of the Lake Huron to Lake Erie Corridor*, 1 https://archive.epa.gov.

23. Nicole Hayden, "Prohibition on Harsens Island," *Port Huron Times Herald*, May 24, 2015, http://www.thetimesherald.com.

24. "The Old Club: Michigan's Best Kept Secret," http://theoldclub.com/.

25. Michigan Department of Environmental Quality, "Great Lakes Bottomland Conveyances," http://www.michigan.gov.

26. US Census Bureau, "Quick Facts, Clay Township, St. Clair County, Michigan," https://www.census.gov/quickfacts/claytownshipstclaircountymichigan.

27. Clay Township, "Phragmites Board," http://www.claytownship.org/departments/phragmities_board/index.php.

Chapter 3. Metropolis Bound

1. All figures are drawn from the Great Lakes Commission's Great Lakes Information Network, http://www.great-lakes.net/lakes/ref/stclfact.html.

2. Http://www.bassresource.com/fishing/st_clair.html.

3. Michigan State University Extension, "Lake St. Clair—a Great North American Fishing Destination," http://msue.anr.msu.edu.

4. Ibid.

5. Terril Yue Jones, "Movement Would Thrust Greatness on Lake St. Clair," *Los Angeles Times*, October 20, 2002.

6. William L. Jenks, *St. Clair County, Michigan, Its History and Its People: A Narrative Account of Its Historical Progress and Its Principal Interests*, vol. 1 (Chicago: Lewis Publishing Co., 1912), 18–19.

7. Mount Clemens Mineral Bath Industry," http://www.michmarkers.com/startup.asp?startpage=L0643.htm.

8. Macomb County government, Macomb County Blue Economy Strategic Development plan, http://ped.macombgov.org/sites/default/files/content/

government/ped/pdfs/MCBluEcoStratDevPlanSec1_9–27–12_1.pdf.

Chapter 4. The Heart of the Lakes

1. John Hartig, "The Return of Detroit River's Charismatic Megafauna," Center for Humans and Nature, November 17, 2014, http://www.humansandnature.org.

2. Allan Carpenter, *Michigan: From Its Glorious Past to the Present* (Chicago: Children's Press, 1964), 12.

3. *Schoolcraft's Narrative Journal of Travels*, ed. Mentor L. Williams (East Lansing: Michigan State University Press, 1992), 53–54.

4. http://www.ste-anne.org/.

5. Albert N. Marquis, ed., *The Book of Detroiters* (Chicago: A.N. Marquis & Co., 1908), 135.

6. Https://www.michmarkers.com/default?page=S0251.

7. Laura Tokie, "With Liberty and Justice for All," *Curator Magazine*, November 13, 2009, http://www.curatormagazine.com/lauratokie/with-liberty-and-justice-for-all/.

8. The route as of the date of this publication is still in the planning stages.

9. Landscape Architecture Foundation, Landscape Performance Series, "William G. Milliken State Park: Phase 2 Lowlands Park," https://landscapeperformance.org/case-study-briefs/milliken-state-park-lowland-park.

10. Victoria P. Ranney, "Frederick Law Olmsted: Designing for Democracy in the Midwest," in *Midwestern Landscape Architecture*, ed. William H. Tishler (Urbana: University of Illinois Press, 2000), 41–55.

11. Michael C. Dempsey, *Castles in the Sand: A City Planner in Abu Dhabi* (Jefferson, NC: McFarland, 2014), 3–4.

12. Jonny Slemrod, "Detroit Groups Work to Exceed Expectations for City," *Michigan Review*, February 7, 2007, 6.

13. "Putting Detroit Back on the Map," *Michigan Daily*, November 18, 2004; "Detroit Sports Stars Make Team to Develop Riverfront Sites," Model D media, February 21, 2006, http://www.modeldmedia.com/devnews/

riverfrnt0221.aspx.

14. Adopted minutes, MEGA Board, (August 15, 2006, 18–19.

15. Dempsey, *Castles in the Sand*, 4.

16. Dennis Archambault, "East Riverfront Investing Guide," *Model D*, March 28, 2006, www.modeldmedia.com/features/erinvesting.aspx.

17. Mothballs being "a condition of protective storage," according to online dictionaries.

18. Clarence M. Burton, William Stocking, and Gordon K. Miller, eds., *The City of Detroit, Michigan, 1701–1922*, vol. 1 (Detroit: S.J. Clarke Publishing Co., 1922), 35.

19. Ibid., 36–37.

20. Ibid., 36.

21. Ibid., 33–34.

22. Amy E. Bragg, *Hidden History of Detroit* (Charleston, SC: History Press, 2011), 115.

23. Burton, Stocking, and Miller, *The City of Detroit*, 8–11.

24. Great Lakes Commission, Maritime in the Great Lakes Region, http://www.great-lakes.net/econ/busenvt/maritime.html#overview.

Chapter 5. Downriver

1. "Living within Questions," *Detroit Metro Times*, June 13, 2007, http://www.metrotimes.com/detroit/living-within-questions/Content?oid=2187503.

2. "The Wonder Well," DownriverThings.com, http://www.downriverthings.com/notable-structures.html.

3. Healthy Lakes.org, "River Clean-Up in Detroit, Michigan Attracts Fish, Wildlife, Economic Development," http://www.healthylakes.org/successes/restoration-success-stories/river-clean-up-in-detroit-michigan-attracts-fish-wildlife-economic-development/.

4. Clarence M. Burton, William Stocking, and Gordon K. Miller, eds. *The City of Detroit, Michigan, 1701–1922*, vol. 2 (Detroit: S.J. Clarke Publishing Co., 1922), 1587.

5. Wyandot of Anderdon Nation, Six Points Master Plan, http://www.

wyandotofanderdon.com/wp/?page_id=385.

6. This convention is an international treaty signed in Ramsar, Iran, in 1971 regarding voluntary international protection of wetlands.

7. John Hartig, personal communication, March 27, 2017.

8. Bill Loomis, "Fishing for a Living in Detroit," *Detroit News*, November 6, 2011.

9. John Knott, ed., *Michigan: Our Land, Our Water, Our Heritage* (Ann Arbor: University of Michigan Press, 2008), 67–72.

10. "An underground body of porous materials, such as sand, gravel, or fractured rock, filled with water and capable of supplying useful quantities of water to a well or spring." http://pubs.usgs.gov/ha/ha747/pdf/definition.pdf.

11. W. H. Sherzer, *Geological Survey of Michigan Lower Peninsula 1896–1900*, vol. 8, part 1, *Geological Report on Monroe County Michigan* (Lansing: Robert Smith Printing Co., 1900), 32.

12. John Knott and Keith Taylor, eds., *The Huron River: Voices from the Watershed* (Ann Arbor: University of Michigan Press, 2000), 14.

13. Ibid., 3.

14. The Huron is the second southeast Michigan trail in the system; St. Clair County's Island Loop, mentioned earlier, was the first.

15. History of the Huron River Chain of Lakes, "Clamming on the Huron," http://historypbw.org/clamming/.

16. Philip P. Mason, *Michigan Highways from Indian Trails to Expressways* (Ann Arbor: Michigan Historical Commission, 1959), 6.

17. Knott and Taylor, *The Huron River*, 15.

18. http://www.michigantrailmaps.com/member-profile/3/21/.

19. Theodore H. Hinchman, *Banks and Banking in Michigan* (Detroit: Wm. Graham, 1887), 39–40.

20. John M. Bulkley, *History of Monroe County Michigan*, vol. 1 (Chicago: Lewis Publishing Co., 1913), 262.

21. Rob Keast, "Who's Who behind Michigan's Named State Parks," *Michigan History* 100, no.2 (March–April 2016): 18.

22. Gerald P. Wykes, "A Strange Silence in Monroe County," *Michigan History* 101, no. 2 (March–April 2017): 29–34.

23. River Raisin Heritage Trail, http://www.rrtrail.com/.

24. Michael D. Moore and William B. Botti, *Michigan's Most Famous and Historic Trees* (Corunna: Michigan Forest Association, 1976), 9.

25. Danielle Portteus, "Visits to the National Battlefield On the Rise," *Monroe News*, January 24, 2017.

26. Danielle Muntz, "River Raisin Watershed Council Finds Larger Partner for Farmer-Led Water Conservation," *Manchester Mirror*, October 31, 2016.

27. Don Faber, *The Toledo War: The First Michigan-Ohio Rivalry* (Ann Arbor: University of Michigan Press, 2008), 178–81.

Epilogue. A Water Legacy

1. Mary Kehoe Smith and Bob Weir, eds., *Explore Our Natural World* (2002), 4.

2. State constitution of 1963, Art. IV, Sec. 52.

3. Business Leaders for Michigan, "The Michigan Natural Resources Business Plan: Leveraging Our Assets to Make Michigan a Top Ten State," July 14, 2015, https://businessleadersformichigan.com.

4. Public Sector Consultants, *Michigan's Water Infrastructure Investment Needs*, April 12, 2016, https://www.publicsectorconsultants.com/wp-content/uploads/2016/12/MI-Water-Infrastructure-Investment-Needs-FINAL-1.pdf.

5. Helen S. Martin, ed., *They Need Not Vanish: A Discussion of the Natural Resources of Michigan* (Lansing: Michigan Department of Conservation, 1942), 187–97.

6. Smith and Weir, *Explore Our Natural World*, 4.

7. Catherine J. Bean, Noel Mullett Jr., and John H. Hartig, "Watershed Planning and Management: The Rouge River Experience," in *Honoring Our Detroit River: Caring for Our Home*, ed. John H. Hartig (Bloomfield Hills, MI: Cranbrook Institute of Science, 2003), 186.

8. Rochelle Riley, *Detroit Free Press*, April 12, 2015.

9. Community Foundation for Southeast Michigan, Greenways Initiative, https://cfsem.org/initiative/greenways-initiative/.

10. Thomas Woiwode, personal communication, April 6, 2017.

BIBLIOGRAPHY

Anderson Economic Group. *Innovating for the Blue Economy: Water Research and Innovation at the URC.* Lansing: University Research Corridor, 2014.

Annin, Peter. *The Great Lakes Water Wars.* Washington, DC: Island Press, 2006.

Ashlee, Laura. *Traveling through Time: A Guide to Michigan's Historical Markers.* Ann Arbor: University of Michigan Press, 2005.

Auer, Nancy, and Dave Dempsey, eds. *The Great Lake Sturgeon.* East Lansing: Michigan State University Press, 2013.

Austin, John, and Alan Steinman. *Michigan Blue Economy: Making Michigan the World's Freshwater & Freshwater Innovation Capital.* Ann Arbor: Michigan Economic Center at Prima Civitas and Grand Valley State University Annis Water Resources Institute, 2014.

Bald, F. Clever. *Michigan in Four Centuries.* New York: Harper & Brothers, 1954.

Botti, William B., and Michael D. Moore. *Michigan's State Forests: A Century of Stewardship.* East Lansing: Michigan State University Press, 2006.

Bragg, Amy E. *Hidden History of Detroit.* Charleston, SC: History Press, 2011.

Burton, Clarence M., William Stocking, and Gordon K. Miller, eds. *The City of Detroit, Michigan, 1701–1922.* Vol. 1. Detroit: S.J. Clarke Publishing Co., 1922.

Business Leaders for Michigan. *Michigan Natural Resources Business Plan: Leveraging Our Assets to Make Michigan a Top Ten State, July 2015.* Lansing: Public Sector Consultants, 2015.

Carpenter, Allan. *Michigan: From Its Glorious Past to the Present.* Chicago: Children's Press, 1964.

Catton, Bruce. *Michigan: A Bicentennial History.* New York: W.W. Norton, 1976.

Cleland, Charles E. *Rites of Conquest: The History and Conquest of Michigan's Native Americans.* Ann Arbor: University of Michigan Press, 1992.

Conway, James, and David F. Jamroz, *Detroit's Historic Fort Wayne.* Charleston, SC: Arcadia Publishing, 2007.

Dennis, Jerry. *The Living Great Lakes: Searching for the Heart of the Inland Seas.* New York: St. Martin's Press, 2004.

Dennis, Jerry, and Craig Date. *Canoeing Michigan Rivers: A Comprehensive Guide to 45 Rivers* Holt, MI: Thunder Bay Press, 2013.

Doner, Mary F. *Blue River.* Garden City, NY: Doubleday, 1946.

Dorr, John A., Jr., and Donald F. Eschman, *Geology of Michigan.* Ann Arbor: University of Michigan Press, 1970.

Dunbar, Willis F. *Michigan: A History of the Wolverine State.* Grand Rapids: William B. Eerdmans, 1970.

Frost, Karolyn S., and Veta S. Tucker, eds. *A Fluid Frontier: Slavery, Resistance, and the Underground Railroad in the Detroit River Borderland.* Detroit: Wayne State University Press, 2016.

Grady, Wayne. *The Great Lakes: The Natural History of a Changing Region.* Vancouver, BC: Greystone Books, 2007.

Halsey, John R. *Beneath the Inland Seas: Michigan's Underwater Archaeological Heritage.* Lansing: Michigan Department of History, Arts and Libraries, 2008.

Hartig, John H. *Bringing Conservation to Cities: Lessons from Building the Detroit River International Wildlife Refuge.* Burlington, ON: Aquatic Ecosystem Health and Management Society, 2014.

Hatcher, Harlan. *Lake Erie.* Indianapolis: Bobbs-Merrill, 1945.

Holling, Holling C. *Paddle-to-the-Sea.* Boston: Houghton Mifflin, 1941.

Knott, John, ed. *Michigan: Our Land, Our Water, Our Heritage.* Ann Arbor: University of Michigan Press, 2008.

Knott, John, and Keith Taylor, eds. *The Huron River: Voices from the Watershed.* Ann Arbor: University of Michigan Press, 2000.

Landon, Fred. *Lake Huron.* Indianapolis: Bobbs-Merrill, 1944.

Manny, Bruce A., Thomas A. Edsall, and Eugene Jaworski. *The Detroit River, Michigan: An Ecological Profile.* Washington, DC: US Fish & Wildlife Service, 1988.

Martin, Helen S., ed. *They Need Not Vanish: A Discussion of the Natural Resources of Michigan.* Lansing: Michigan Department of Conservation, 1942.

Mason, Philip P. *Michigan Highways from Indian Trails to Expressways.* Ann Arbor: Michigan Historical Commission, 1959.

May, George S. *Pictorial History of Michigan.* Grand Rapids: William B. Eerdmans, 1967–69.

McDonnell, Michael A. *Masters of Empire: Great Lakes Indians and the Making of America.* New York: Hill and Wang, 2015.

Moore, Michael D., and William B. Botti, *Michigan's Most Famous and Historic Trees.* Corunna: Michigan Forest Association, 1976.

Munawar, M., and R. Heath, eds. *Checking the Pulse of Lake Erie.* Burlington, ON: Aquatic Ecosystem Health and Management Society, 2008.

———, eds. *The Lake Huron Ecosystem: Ecology, Fisheries and Management* Burlington, ON: Aquatic Ecosystem Health and Management Society, 1995.

O'Connor, Ryan P., Michael A. Kost, and Joshua G. Cohen. *Prairies and Savannas in Michigan: Rediscovering Our Natural Heritage.* East Lansing: Michigan State University Press, 2009.

Peters, Scott M. *Making Waves: Michigan's Boat-Building Industry, 1865–2000.* Ann Arbor: University of Michigan Press, 2015.

Ranney, Victoria P. "Frederick Law Olmsted: Designing for Democracy in the Midwest." In *Midwestern Landscape Architecture,* edited by William H. Tishler, 41–55. Urbana: University of Illinois Press, 2000.

Romig, Walter. *Michigan Place Names: The History of the Founding and the Naming of More Than Five Thousand Past and Present Michigan Communities.* Detroit:

Wayne State University Press, 1986.

Royce, Julia A. *Traveling Michigan's Thumb: Exploring a Shoreline of Small Pleasures and Unexpected Treasures.* Indianapolis: Dog Ear Publishing, 2006.

Rubenstein, Bruce A., and Lawrence E. Ziewacz. *Michigan: A History of the Great Lakes State.* Wheeling, IL: Harlan Davidson, 2008.

Santer, Richard A. *Michigan: Heart of the Great Lakes.* Dubuque: Kendall/Hunt Publishing, 1977.

Schoolcraft, Henry R. *Narrative Journal of Travels through the Northwestern Regions of the United States Extending from Detroit through the Great Chain of American Lakes to the Sources of the Mississippi River in the Year 1820.* Edited by Mentor L. Williams. East Lansing: Michigan State University Press, 1953.

Shiawassee & Huron: Headwaters Resource Preservation Project: A Unique Setting Worth Preserving. Ann Arbor, MI: Carlisle Wortman & Assoc., 2000.

Smith, Mary Kehoe, and Bob Weir, eds., *Explore Our Natural World: A Biodiversity Atlas of the Lake Huron to Lake Erie Corridor.* N.p.: n.p., 2002.

Sommers, Lawrence M., ed. *Atlas of Michigan.* East Lansing: Michigan State University Press, 1977.

Swan, Alison, ed. *Fresh Water: Women Writing on the Great Lakes.* East Lansing: Michigan State University Press, 2006.

Taylor, Paul. *"Old Slow Town": Detroit during the Civil War.* Detroit: Wayne State University Press, 2013.

Thurtell, Joel. *Up the Rouge! Paddling Detroit's Hidden River.* Detroit: Wayne State University Press, 2009.

Vachon, Paul. *Forgotten Detroit.* Charleston, SC: Arcadia Publishing, 2009.

Willard, Nancy. *Sister Water.* New York: Alfred A. Knopf, 1993.

Woodford, Frank B. *Mr. Jefferson's Disciple: A Life of Justice Woodward.* East Lansing: Michigan State College Press, 1953.

Works Progress Administration. *Michigan: A Guide to the Wolverine State.* New York: Oxford University Press, 1956.